LEADING THE
Technology-Powered
SCHOOL

LEADING THE
Technology-Powered
SCHOOL

MARILYN L.
GRADY

CORWIN
A SAGE Company

CORWIN
A SAGE Company

FOR INFORMATION:

Corwin

A SAGE Company

2455 Teller Road

Thousand Oaks, California 91320

(800) 233-9936

Fax: (800) 417-2466

www.corwin.com

SAGE Ltd.

1 Oliver's Yard

55 City Road

London EC1Y 1SP

United Kingdom

SAGE India Pvt. Ltd.

B 1/I 1 Mohan Cooperative Industrial Area

Mathura Road, New Delhi 110 044

India

SAGE Asia-Pacific Pte. Ltd.

33 Pekin Street #02-01

Far East Square

Singapore 048763

Acquisitions Editor: Debra Stollenwerk

Associate Editor: Desirée A. Bartlett

Editorial Assistant: Kimberly Greenberg

Production Editor: Amy Schroller

Typesetter: C&M Digitals (P) Ltd.

Proofreader: Gail Fay

Indexer: Michael Ferreira

Cover Designer: Scott Van Atta

Permissions Editor: Adele Hutchinson

Printed in the United States of America

Library of Congress Cataloging-in-Publication Data

Grady, Marilyn L.

Leading the technology-powered school/ Marilyn L. Grady.

p. cm.
Includes bibliographical references.

ISBN 978-1-4129-4948-4 (pbk.)

1. Educational technology—United States.
2. Educational leadership—United States. I. Title.

LB1028.3.G723 2011 371.330973—dc22 2011001805

This book is printed on acid-free paper.

11 12 13 14 15 10 9 8 7 6 5 4 3 2 1

Contents

Acknowledgments   vii

About the Author   ix

Introduction: Through the Eyes of the Five-Year-Old   1
    A Book for Busy Principals   1
    Special Features   2
    Organization   3
    21st Century Learning   3

PART I: HUMAN CAPITAL   5

1. The Principal as Technology Leader   7
    Vision and Goals   8
    Support Technology Use   10
    Professional Development   11
    Resources   17

2. Teachers: The Magic Link Between
    Technology and Students   31
    Incentives   31
    Technology Use   32
    Generational Shift   34
    Resources   41

3. The Technology Leadership Team   45
    The Technology Specialist   45
    The Technology Leadership Team   50
    Resources   55

PART II: CORE ISSUES   59

4. Professional Development: The
    Teacher-to-Teacher Approach   61
    Stages of Concern   62
    Teacher to Teacher   65

	Professional Development Agenda	65
	Need Based	67
	Administrator Involvement	68
5.	**Cybersafety Leadership: Guarding the Borders**	**69**
	Boundaries	70
	Risks and Challenges	70
	Filtering or Not?	71
	Cybersafety Leadership	73
	Resources	79
6.	**Assessment: Technology Use and Skills**	**83**
	Technology Assessment	83
	Formative Evaluation	84
	Classroom Assessments	86
	Assessment Challenges	87
	Teachers' Use of Technology	87
	Principals' Use of Technology	88
	Digital Age Assessment	88
	PART III: QUESTIONS AND REFLECTIONS	**91**
7.	**Questions and Reflections**	**93**
	Technology Trends	95
	References	**99**
	Index	**103**

Acknowledgments

Justin Grady provided fine support throughout the writing process. Although he is many miles away, he kindly inquired about *the book* each time I talked to him and never questioned, "How long is this going to take?" Elizabeth Grady exercised infinite patience on the home front as I continued to redistribute the book pages throughout our house. I am thankful for their support.

The book is enriched by the experiences and expertise of principals, superintendents, librarians, media specialists, and technology specialists. I am thankful for the perspectives they shared with me during interview sessions.

Minisa Chapman-Huls provided excellent research assistance throughout the writing process. Suzanne Becking provided assistance in the preparation of the manuscript. I am thankful for their skills and good humor.

Everyone who writes should have the benefit of an outstanding editor. I am thankful for Corwin editor Debra Stollenwerk.

Peer reviewers of an earlier version of the book manuscript provided many valuable and thoughtful comments. I am thankful for their attention to the manuscript and their insights.

PUBLISHER'S ACKNOWLEDGMENTS

Corwin gratefully acknowledges the following individuals for their editorial insight:

Nathan Flansburg, Principal
Valentine Hills Elementary School
Arden Hills, Minnesota

Nancy Fuller, Director of School Improvement and Curriculum
Auburn Public Schools
Auburn, Nebraska

About the Author

Marilyn L. Grady, PhD, is a professor of educational administration at the University of Nebraska–Lincoln (UNL). She is the author or coauthor of 23 books, including *From Difficult Teachers to Dynamic Teamwork* (2009) with Brock, *Getting It Right From the Start* (2009) with Kostelnik, *From First Year to First Rate* (2007) with Brock, *194 High-Impact Letters for Busy Principals* (2006), *20 Biggest Mistakes Principals Make and How to Avoid Them* (2004), and *Launching Your First Principalship* (2004) with Brock. Her research areas include leadership, the principalship, and superintendent-board relations. She has more than 175 publications to her credit. She is the editor of the *Journal of Women in Educational Leadership.* Her editorial board service has included *Educational Administration Quarterly, International Studies in Educational Administration, International Journal of Learning, Rural Educator, Journal of At-Risk Issues, Journal of School Leadership, Journal for Rural School and Community Renewal, Journal for a Just and Caring Education,* and the online publication *Advancing Women in Leadership Journal.* She is the recipient of the Stanley Brzezinski Research Award, the NCPEA (National Council of Professors of Educational Administration) Living Legend Award, the Donald R. and Mary Lee Swanson Award for Teaching Excellence, UNL's Distinguished Teaching Award, and UNL's Award for Outstanding Contributions to the Status of Women.

Dr. Grady coordinates an annual conference on women in educational leadership that attracts national attendance and is in its 25th year. She has been an administrator in K–12 schools as well as at the college and university levels. She received her bachelor's degree in history from Saint Mary's College, Notre Dame, Indiana, and her doctorate in educational administration with a specialty in leadership from The Ohio State University. Her email address is mgrady1@unl.edu.

This book is dedicated to the youngest of my children, Elizabeth.

Elizabeth "gets" writing.

I hope she will continue to write throughout her life with the same joy and enthusiasm she has today.

Introduction

Through the Eyes of the Five-Year-Old

I thought it was funny when my daughter called me the night that my grandson started kindergarten. She woke up at 6:30 that morning, went down the hall to his bedroom, and he was gone. She looked through the house. She found him all dressed in his little kindergarten outfit, his backpack beside the chair, and he was at the computer doing stuff. And I'm thinking, this is five—this is a five-year-old for Pete's sake. So it's just different. And so the idea of kids sitting there quietly, listening to somebody lecture them, is not going to work. They need that instant feedback, and I don't think that we can give it to them. The technology is going to have to help us provide that. These are the kids who are coming to school.

For those who have been slow, or reluctant, to embrace technology or become proficient in its use and application in schools, the time is now—now is the time to meet the students where they are.

Technology has been available in school settings for 30 years. In many places, the available technology has not been used or implemented in the instructional life of the school. Often the reason for this has been a lack of interest, motivation, and leadership. However, when the students come to school more proficient with technology than the school leaders, it is time for a transformation in school practices.

A BOOK FOR BUSY PRINCIPALS

The chapters in the book are derived from the literature on leadership; technology; the roles of principals, teachers, technology specialists, and the technology leadership team; professional development; cybersafety; and assessment.

The book features strategies principals can use to enhance their work as leaders of technology in schools. A number of resources are provided to extend the usefulness of the book. Websites and blogs are listed with the advice to the principal: Spend 15 minutes a day in exploration. The websites provide easily accessible professional development for the busy principal.

The book is not a technology book; it is a leadership book. It is written from an understanding of the many roles principals must assume and the time constraints they experience in their work. The focus is on what principals can accomplish on a daily and weekly basis to facilitate the use of technology in the school. Technology is viewed as a tool that can enhance instruction. The book is written with an understanding that changes in technology are constant.

My experiences as a principal, university administrator, and professor inform my approach to the topic of leadership and technology. My earliest experiences with integrating computers into instruction occurred at the University of Illinois, Urbana-Champaign, on Plato (Programmed Logic for Automated Teaching Operations). At that time, I was a coordinator of instructional development.

SPECIAL FEATURES

Voices of School Leaders

The voices of school leaders are a special feature of the book. Interviews were conducted with principals, assistant principals, associate superintendents, curriculum leaders, technology coordinators, teachers, librarians, and media specialists. These individuals' voices are reflected in the chapters. The voices are represented by a microphone icon throughout the text. The book provides school leaders with a mirror in the form of the voices of school leaders who offer their stories and suggestions. These vignettes reflect the real world of the school.

Resources

Extensive resources support the text. Website addresses provide busy school leaders with resources at their fingertips. Checklists and surveys provide self-assessment and school-assessment tools that support the work of school leaders.

Principal's Exploration Agenda

The book is written from the perspective that principals are very busy. With this in mind, the book offers a "Principal's Exploration Agenda" that encourages principals to take 15 minutes a day to build capacity by exploring the vast resources related to technology.

Action Agenda

Chapters 1 through 6 conclude with an action agenda to guide follow-up activities. The emphasis is on moving beyond the text to actions that will enhance the principal's leadership of technology in the school. Practical strategies are emphasized.

ORGANIZATION

The book has three parts. Part I focuses on human capital: the principal, the teachers, the technology specialists, and the technology leadership team. These individuals are essential to implementation of technology in the school. Part II focuses on three core tasks: professional development, cybersafety, and assessment. These tasks are critical for principals who are leaders of technology. Part III includes questions and reflections.

21ST CENTURY LEARNING

Students' lives are linked to the media and technology tools available to them. Students in schools are digital learners. Cell phones, MP3 players, handheld gaming devices, PDAs, and laptops are part of their daily lives. Social networking through Facebook, Twitter, and MySpace is common. Even toddlers use gaming devices such as Leapster and websites such as www.PBSkids.org and www.nick.com (What Is 21st Century Education? 2004).

Classroom activities that support acquisition of these skills include active learning, integrated and interdisciplinary curriculum, and project-based and problem-based learning. Many forms of media and technology support these learning activities.

Throughout the book, the comments of school leaders reinforce the link between 21st Century skills and the use of technology. Information, media, and technology skills are essential components of "21st Century Student Outcomes and Support Systems" (in Partnership for 21st Century Skills, 2009, para.1).

Principal leadership in the 21st Century school demands leadership in technology. The principal must meet the five-year-old at the schoolhouse door.

Part I
Human Capital

1 The Principal as Technology Leader

The effective 21st Century administrator is a hands-on user of technology.

TSSA Collaborative (2001, p. 4).

The principal's diverse roles are part of a long tradition of expectations and responsibilities. Of recent vintage is the role of principal as technology leader. The special challenge for the principal is being a technology leader as well as encouraging the development of teacher and student technology leaders.

The "insider" secret principals know: The technology came first and the principal as technology leader came later. Preparation experiences for the principal's role as technology leader may be absent or fragmented. Often technology knowledge and skills are "learned by doing."

The principal's role as technology leader includes the following 10 tasks:

1. The principal should establish the vision and goals for technology in the school.

2. The principal should carry the technology banner in the school.

3. The principal should model use of technology.

4. The principal should support technology use in the school.

5. The principal should engage in professional development activities that focus on technology and integration of technology in student learning activities.

6. The principal should provide professional development opportunities for teachers and staff that emphasize use of technology and that facilitate integration of technology into student learning.

7. The principal should secure resources to support technology use and integration in the school.

8. The principal should be an advocate for technology use that supports student learning.

9. The principal should be knowledgeable and supportive of national technology standards and promote attainment of the standards in the school. (See "Resources" for Technology Standards for School Administrators and the Draft National Education Technology Plan 2010.)

10. The principal should communicate the uses and importance of technology in enhancing student learning experiences to the school's stakeholders.

Remember: Technology is nothing more than tools used to complete work.

VISION AND GOALS

The principal must establish the vision and goals for technology in the school. The principal carries the vision "banner" and promotes the vision throughout the school (Grady & LeSourd, 1989–1990; LeSourd & Grady, 1989–1990; LeSourd, Tracz, & Grady, 1992). All who work in the school strive to achieve the vision. "In the visionary role, principals establish a context for technology in the school and understand how technology can be used to restructure learning environments and empower teachers and students to be technologically astute" (Brockmeier, Sermon, & Hope, p. 46). Principals must use their "leadership to step up the pace, and create the sense of urgency, vision and strategic plan" (Technology & Learning, n.d., p. 4).

The vision includes the following:

- The leadership the principal exerts on technology integration into the teaching and learning process
- The role of teachers in integration of technology into teaching and learning activities
- The standards that will guide the technology plan for the school
- The measures that will be applied to assess technology use
- The resources that are necessary to enable effective use of technology by students and teachers
- The communication with families and community members to showcase the use of technology to facilitate student learning and achievement

Trotter (1997) states, "Set your goals first, then consider tools. Otherwise, technology vendors will urge you to adopt goals that fit what they have to sell. . . . You don't want to buy a technology solution. You want to help design a functional solution" (p. 5).

Model the Use of Technology

Principals who are comfortable with technology become models of technology use in schools. If the goal is to encourage teachers and staff members to use technology, then the principal is the key figure in its adoption and use (Brockmeier, Sermon, & Hope, 2005; Cooley & Reitz, 1997).

Johnson (2005) describes a principal who implemented the six Technology Standards for School Administrators (TSSA). In the example, the high school principal's actions demonstrate how technology use is modeled by a principal. For instance, the principal demonstrated meeting the Productivity and Professional Practice standard by communicating "regularly and effectively to staff, parents, and community using email, listservs, and websites. . . . His school board reports are illustrated with graphs and photos embedded in multimedia presentations. He uses districtwide calendar programs for facilities scheduling and managing his own schedule" (p. 1).

In another example, the principal demonstrated meeting the Support, Management, and Operations standard:

> Using the student information system, [the principal] tracks the day-to-day operations of the school through ready access to schedules, attendance records, health records, discipline incidents, grades, and online teacher grade books. He carries most of this in his personal digital assistant, synchronized with his desktop computer. He manages his building budget using the district's real-time finance program (Johnson, 2005, p. 1).

In these examples, the principal uses technology to accomplish the management tasks of the school. Through consistent, daily use that touches the academic, behavioral, administrative, and supervisory aspects of the school, teachers, staff, students, and parents have clear evidence of the principal's use of technology. One principal reported using a Goggle Apps–based calendar so that the staff and teachers could access the calendar and post information on the calendar as well.

Principals need to be knowledgeable of the technology standards and use these as a basis of action in the school. "An underlying assumption in these standards [TSSA] is that administrators should be competent users of information and technology tools common to information-age professionals" (TSSA Collaborative, 2001, p. 4).

To model technology use, principals must learn to use the technology tools that are available. By adopting the technology and using it at home and at the office, a principal can learn "to think beyond the individual bits of equipment to lessons about how technology can shape and serve an overall system of education" (Trotter, 1997, p. 5).

SUPPORT TECHNOLOGY USE

To be a technology leader involves many of the leadership skills principals display in other aspects of their work. Technology leadership demands attention to technology use throughout the school. The vision for technology use includes a commitment to this focus.

Following are actions principals can take as technology leaders.

Showcase Technology Use

Staff Meetings. As a principal, it is critical to focus on the vision and goals of the school. If the vision calls for technology integration throughout the curriculum, then examples of technology use must be showcased. One precious resource in schools is time. If principals focus attention on technology use during the limited time available for staff meetings, then all in attendance will understand that technology use in the classroom is valued. Provide brief demonstrations of technology integration in different grades or subject areas. Whenever staff meetings are held, a small portion of the meeting should be used for these demonstrations.

These sessions should emphasize both technology integration into student learning activities and how technology enhances student learning. Student projects can be showcased. Specific lessons can be highlighted. Teacher teams or subject-area specialists can feature integrated projects that present technology use. Make these brief demonstrations a regular feature of staff meetings so that all will anticipate this segment of the meeting. By consistency in featuring technology, teachers will be motivated to demonstrate their technology use during this designated time. These opportunities will deliver the message that technology integration is a goal that will be achieved in the school.

Prominent Displays. Photos that feature student and classroom use of technology spread the word that technology is an important aspect of lesson delivery and demonstration. When the photos are displayed throughout the school, families, teachers, community members, and visitors receive the message that technology is a vibrant part of the school. Students and teachers whose work is featured in the photos take pride in their accomplishments and look forward to being part of the photo displays.

Remember: At the beginning of the school year, secure signed permission or release forms from parents or guardians for the use of student photos in the various media outlets used by the school.

Remember: As principal, you have access to all the learning and activity areas of the school. Use the access you have to capture pictures that reflect all school areas. Keep the camera with you!

Develop a schedule for updating photo displays so that they continue to attract the attention of those who pass through the school. Develop the schedule with the faculty and staff. Enlist their help in contributing photos of students, special events, and classroom activities. Classes can be assigned specific weeks for their displays. The showcase should emphasize standards-based learning completed through the use of technology. The technology can include a variety of the formats accessible to students. Posters, digital pictures, PowerPoints, and digital movies can be featured.

Identify themes for the displays that reflect the academic, athletic, and performance aspects of the school. Use the seasons of the year, as well as national holidays, as additional themes for photo displays.

Feature technology use on the school website. Alert teachers, students, and families to the website. Feature photos and movie clips. Visitors will be drawn to other important information about the school through these visuals. Use technology to improve communication throughout the school community.

Install a monitor in the entryway to the school and stream photos and movie clips. Students, parents, and teachers take pride in the photos, and all who pass through the entrance will be alerted to school activities and technology's uses in the school.

PROFESSIONAL DEVELOPMENT

Professional Development: Technology

The most important resources in the school are the human resources or human capital (Figure 1.1). These individuals must be a central focus for the principal.

Professional development is essential to enhancing the skills of teachers, staff, and administrators. Principals should use these opportunities to achieve the vision and goals of the school. Often, professional development is left in the hands of outside experts or is expected to occur through conference

Figure 1.1 Human Capital in the School

Human Capital

- Students
- Librarian
- Media specialist
- Technology specialist
- Teachers
- Staff

attendance. Unfortunately, the outside experts and conferences may not provide the knowledge and skills needed to achieve the school's goals. Principals need to use professional development as part of their leadership of the school. These experiences are critical to achieving school goals and should be aligned with the vision and goals of the school. The principal must maintain constant oversight of this critical resource.

Provide a series of professional development sessions that focus on common and new technologies. Select technology tools that are easily applied to the teaching and learning that occur at each grade level. Whenever possible, ask a teacher to model the technology for the teachers. Focus the experiences on subject areas, teams, interdisciplinary teams, or department-level groupings. Demonstrate the technology as it is applied in a specific subject lesson or activity. Provide examples of students' use of the technology in completing specific classroom activities. Record the sessions so that teachers can review them after the events. Move away from the "one time" approach to demonstrations and adopt the "repeat, repeat, repeat" approach.

Invite different teachers to showcase technology so that all teachers become leaders of technology use. These practices will reduce resistance to technology use and will encourage development of additional technology skills. Identify the tech-savvy teachers in the school (Figure 1.2).

Figure 1.2 Tech-Savvy Teachers in the School

Tech-Savvy Teachers

Have you identified the tech savvy in the school?

Who, among these groups, is underutilized?

What skills do these individuals have that may be better utilized in the school?

New technology tools appear and change at a rapid pace. The tools that were new at the beginning of the school year may be enhanced, transformed, or replaced by the end of the school year. Teachers need to be in a constant cycle of exposure to and implementation of new technologies. Acceptance of and comfort with these continuous changes will be facilitated by frequent, brief exposure to the new modalities. The teacher-to-teacher model will continue to be the ideal means of reducing resistance to change. Rogers (2003), in *Diffusion of Innovations,* reports on a number of successful change implementations. Essential to the success of these innovations was the person-to-person or peer-to-peer dimension of the changes. As the cycle of teacher demonstrations continues, teachers will refer to the process as "this is the way we do things in this school."

Figure 1.3 Technology Implementation Leadership Model

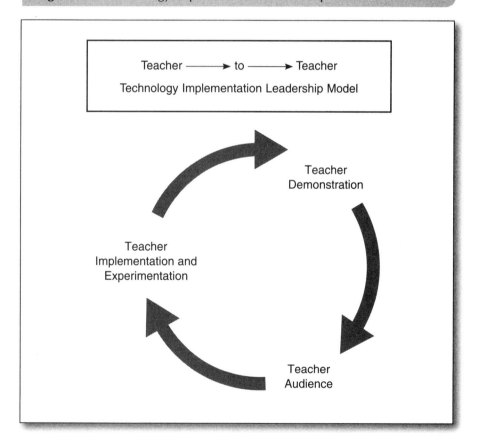

Incorporate technology demonstration and implementation as part of the teacher appraisal process. As you engage in teacher observations, note students' use of technology in class work as well as teachers' integration of technology into instruction. Recognize these practices in your observation notes and convey this recognition to the teachers. Establish goals with teachers for their development of technology skills. Encourage implementation of technology in instructional strategies. As you review lesson plans, note teachers' use of technology throughout the lessons. Recognition of technology use will reinforce its inclusion in the instructional process.

Professional Development: Student Learning

As part of professional development activities, provide opportunities for teachers to use technology tools to track student achievement and attainment of learning goals. Use the teacher-to-teacher model of demonstrating these tools. Demonstrate how the technology tools can be used to report student progress to parents and guardians. The progress reports can include students' attainment of instructional goals as well as academic progress in the subject areas. A calendar can be developed as part of a regular plan for communication with parents and guardians. Demonstrate technology tools that present student data through a variety of graphs and models so that students' accomplishments can be routinely reported. Provide opportunities for teachers to learn and practice the use of these tools. Establish timelines for implementation of these tools. Recognize teachers as they gain expertise. Visit with teachers about their plans to develop strategies with students who are not meeting the standards or expectations.

Professional Development: Principals

Make your own professional development a priority. Consider the following professional development activities as a means of enhancing your technology skills and leadership:

- ✓ Attend the annual state technology conference and become familiar with new technology uses and resources. For the annual conference, present a session on administrative uses of technology or on strategies for encouraging technology integration into teaching and learning activities. Become a leader in the state technology association.
- ✓ Present sessions at state and national conferences for teachers and administrators. Through these presentations, you will advance your knowledge of your subject and increase your network of colleagues. You meet more people through your role as presenter than you do through passive attendance at conference sessions. The conversations that emerge from your presentation advance your thinking and can link you to others who share your professional interests.

✓ Model and practice the use of technology in your presentations. If you want teachers to use technology, you must model the use of technology. As you become more accomplished in the use and application of technology, you will be better able to understand the reservations and challenges teachers may experience.

✓ Attend training sessions on the use and applications of new technologies. Practice the use of these resources so that you are able to discuss them with the technology coordinator as well as teachers. Identify training opportunities for teachers through attendance at these sessions.

Provide Resources

The principal's role is to secure resources to support the use and integration of technology in the school. Resources include examples of technology use and integration as well as hardware, software, and other equipment to support technology use. The principal should provide a steady stream of examples of technology use and innovation. These examples should focus on the various academic areas and should be made available to all of the teachers. Principals receive a constant barrage of email blasts, newsletters, webinar invitations, and journals that report technology innovations in school districts throughout the United States. By sharing or distributing examples of technology innovation and use, individual teachers may find a source of inspiration for their subject area. In the spirit of Rogers' (2003) work on diffusion of innovations, the teacher-to-teacher examples of technology integration may have the greatest valence for motivating reluctant adopters of technology use and integration.

Remember: Cooley and Reitz (1997) concluded that the principal more than any other educator is key to teachers' adoption and use of technology.

National Technology Standards

Principals must be knowledgeable of the national technology standards and use the standards in the school. "The Collaborative for Technology Standards for School Administrators (TSSA Collaborative) has facilitated the development of a national consensus on what P–12 administrators should know and be able to do to optimize the effective use of technology" (p. 3).

The Technology Standards for School Administrators (TSSA Collaborative, 2001) are included in "Resources" for this chapter. In addition, an excerpt from the National Education Technology Plan 2010 (Office of Educational Technology, 2010) is included. These resources provide guidance as schools refine their implementation and integration of technology throughout the school, curriculum, and teaching and learning process.

A Word on Leadership

➢ Model the use of technology: If you use it, they use it.

➢ Remember, all eyes are on you: They see everything you do.

➢ Speak no disparaging words: They hear everything you say.

➢ Recall that one word from the principal makes all the difference: They are waiting for your encouraging words.

➢ Conduct one-legged interviews: Check on implementation progress.

➢ Celebrate successes: Set benchmarks and cheer accomplishments.

➢ Create a culture of experimentation and risk taking: Small increments of progress matter.

➢ Practice makes perfect: Hands on, again and again and again.

➢ Remember: It isn't a one-time purchase.

➢ Make time and take time to play and learn.

➢ Provide money and resources: Acquire the necessary hardware, software, and training.

Source: Adapted from Grady (2004).

ACTION AGENDA

• Invite teachers to showcase use of technology at faculty meetings.
• Display examples of student technology use throughout the school.
• Follow the principal's exploration agenda: Explore the technology resources using the 15-minute-a-day approach.

Resources

Principal Self-Assessment

Principal's Exploration Agenda

Technology Standards for School Administrators

Excerpt From the Draft National Education Technology Plan 2010

PRINCIPAL SELF-ASSESSMENT

Figure 1.4 Principal Self-Assessment

Complete the principal self-assessment as an additional tool for professional development:

Principal Tasks (Check)	YES (✓)	NO (✓)
Are the vision and goals for technology displayed in the school?		
Do you model technology use?		
Do you take actions that demonstrate support for technology use?		
Do you annually attend professional development activities focused on technology?		
Are professional development opportunities focused on technology use and integration offered annually for faculty and staff?		
Do you provide resources for teachers and staff that support technology use and integration throughout the school?		
Do you advocate for technology use in support of student learning?		
Do you support the attainment of national technology standards in the school?		
Do you communicate with stakeholders about the use and importance of technology in enhancing student learning?		

PRINCIPAL'S EXPLORATION AGENDA

Use the 15-minute-a-day approach to explore the vast resources related to technology. This short time frame will provide a valuable professional development experience. The following sites are places to begin the exploration.

 RSS Feeds: Rich Site Summary, commonly referred to as *Really Simple Syndication,* is a format for delivering web content such as news sites, blogs, and other online publications. RSS feeds are similar to a subscription only easier to use.

RSS solves a problem for busy people who regularly use the web. It allows you to quickly stay informed by retrieving the latest content from the sites you are interested in. You save time by bringing the news to you rather than searching several sites daily.

The only thing you need to use RSS feeds is a newsreader such as My Yahoo! or Google Reader. When you find a blog or a webpage you want to read regularly, simply click on the RSS feed icon (like the icon in the preceding text) and choose the reader you would like to use.

Blogs

- Dangerously Irrelevant: A blog site for sharing thoughts for K–12 educators, highlighting technology and leadership with a vision for the future of education, is led by Scott McLeod, codirector of CASTLE (UCEA Center for the Advanced Study of Technology Leadership in Education):

  http://www.dangerouslyirrelevant.org

- Doug Johnson's Blue Skunk Blog: Blue Skunk Blog was created to provide a convenient way for people to respond to Johnson's writing and presentations:

  http://doug-johnson.squarespace.com

- Education Week: This blog is focused on technology and trends in education:

  http://blogs.edweek.org/edweek/DigitalEducation

- Education Week: Leader Talk: A CASTLE project. This blog is focused on the school leader:

  http://blogs.edweek.org/edweek/LeaderTalk

- Tech & Learning: This blog features topics for K–12 educators:

  http://www.techlearning.com/section/Blogs

- Typepad: This blog was created by the Association for Supervision and Curriculum Development for the K–12 educators:

  http://www.ascd.typepad.com/blog

Resource Sites

- Cybersmart: This site emphasizes 21st Century skills:

  http://www.cybersmart.org

- Cyber Security for the Digital District: The site provides tools for K–12 technology leaders:

  http://www.cosn.org/cybersecurity

- Eduweb: This site provides learning games and interactive activities for students:

  http://www.eduweb.com

- eSchool News: This site provides technology news for educators of K–20:

  http://www.eschoolnews.com

- International Society for Technology in Education: ISTE provides technology standards for students, teachers, and school administrators:

  http://www.iste.org/standards.aspx

- iTunes U: This site allows educators to search for digital educational content for students:

  http://www.apple.com/education/itunes-u

- Launchy: This site offers an open-source keystroke launcher to launch programs and files quickly from your desktop:

  http://www.launchy.net

- Phrase Express: This site allows you to create abbreviations for short phrases; call up the abbreviations and it will finish typing the phrase for you:

  http://www.phraseexpress.com

- Renaissance Learning: This site provides advanced technology resources for educators:

  http://www.renlearn.com/neo/NEO2/default.aspx

- SchoolTube: This site allows students and teachers to share videos online:

  http://www.schooltube.com

- Tech Smith: This site offers free and paid software downloads for screen capture and voice-over:

  http://www.techsmith.com

- THE Journal: This site provides K–12 news and resources for educators:

  http://thejournal.com/Home.aspx

TECHNOLOGY STANDARDS FOR SCHOOL ADMINISTRATORS

I. Leadership and Vision

Educational leaders inspire a shared vision for comprehensive integration of technology and foster an environment and culture conducive to the realization of that vision.

Educational leaders

A. facilitate the shared development by all stakeholders of a vision for technology use and widely communicate that vision.

B. maintain an inclusive and cohesive process to develop, implement, and monitor a dynamic, long-range, and systemic technology plan to achieve the vision.

C. foster and nurture a culture of responsible risk-taking and advocate policies promoting continuous innovation with technology.

D. use data in making leadership decisions.

E. advocate for research-based effective practices in use of technology.

F. advocate, on the state and national levels, for policies, programs, and funding opportunities that support implementation of the district technology plan.

II. Learning and Teaching

Educational leaders ensure that curricular design, instructional strategies, and learning environments integrate appropriate technologies to maximize learning and teaching.

Educational leaders

A. identify, use, evaluate, and promote appropriate technologies to enhance and support instruction and standards-based curriculum leading to high levels of student achievement.

B. facilitate and support collaborative technology-enriched learning environments conducive to innovation for improved learning.

C. provide for learner-centered environments that use technology to meet the individual and diverse needs of learners.

D. facilitate the use of technologies to support and enhance instructional methods that develop higher-level thinking, decision-making, and problem-solving skills.

E. provide for and ensure that faculty and staff take advantage of quality professional learning opportunities for improved learning and teaching with technology.

III. Productivity and Professional Practice

Educational leaders apply technology to enhance their professional practice and to increase their own productivity and that of others.

Educational leaders

A. model the routine, intentional, and effective use of technology.

B. employ technology for communication and collaboration among colleagues, staff, parents, students, and the larger community.

C. create and participate in learning communities that stimulate, nurture, and support faculty and staff in using technology for improved productivity.

D. engage in sustained, job-related professional learning using technology resources.

E. maintain awareness of emerging technologies and their potential uses in education.

F. use technology to advance organizational improvement.

FRAMEWORK, STANDARDS, AND PERFORMANCE INDICATORS

IV. Support, Management, and Operations

Educational leaders ensure the integration of technology to support productive systems for learning and administration.

Educational leaders

A. develop, implement, and monitor policies and guidelines to ensure compatibility of technologies.

B. implement and use integrated technology-based management and operations systems.

C. allocate financial and human resources to ensure complete and sustained implementation of the technology plan.

D. integrate strategic plans, technology plans, and other improvement plans and policies to align efforts and leverage resources.

E. implement procedures to drive continuous improvements of technology systems and to support technology replacement cycles.

V. Assessment and Evaluation

Educational leaders use technology to plan and implement comprehensive systems of effective assessment and evaluation.

Educational leaders

A. use multiple methods to assess and evaluate appropriate uses of technology resources for learning, communication, and productivity.

B. use technology to collect and analyze data, interpret results, and communicate findings to improve instructional practice and student learning.

C. assess staff knowledge, skills, and performance in using technology and use results to facilitate quality professional development and to inform personnel decisions.

D. use technology to assess, evaluate, and manage administrative and operational systems.

VI. Social, Legal, and Ethical Issues

Educational leaders understand the social, legal, and ethical issues related to technology and model responsible decision making related to these issues.

Educational leaders

A. ensure equity of access to technology resources that enable and empower all learners and educators.

B. identify, communicate, model, and enforce social, legal, and ethical practices to promote responsible use of technology.

C. promote and enforce privacy, security, and online safety related to the use of technology.

D. promote and enforce environmentally safe and healthy practices in the use of technology.

E. participate in the development of policies that clearly enforce copyright law and assign ownership of intellectual property developed with district resources.

Source: This material was originally produced as a project of the Technology Standards for School Administrators Collaborative (2010, pp. 6–7), www.ncrtec.org/pd/tssa/tssa.pdf. Used with permission, April 2010.

EXCERPT FROM THE DRAFT NATIONAL EDUCATION TECHNOLOGY PLAN 2010

Goals and Recommendations

The NETP presents five goals with recommendations for states, districts, the federal government, and other stakeholders in our education system that address learning, assessment, teaching, infrastructure, and productivity. The plan also identifies far-reaching grand challenge problems that should be funded and coordinated at a national level.

1.0 Learning

All learners will have engaging and empowering learning experiences both in and outside of school that prepare them to be active, creative, knowledgeable, and ethical participants in our globally networked society.

To meet this goal, we recommend the following actions:

1.1 Revise, create, and adopt standards and learning objectives for all content areas that reflect 21st century expertise and the power of technology to improve learning.

1.2 Develop and adopt learning resources that use technology to embody design principles from the learning sciences.

1.3 Develop and adopt learning resources that exploit the flexibility and power of technology to reach all learners anytime and anywhere.

1.4 Use advances in the learning sciences and technology to enhance STEM (science, technology, engineering, and mathematics) learning and develop, adopt, and evaluate new methodologies with the potential to enable all learners to excel in STEM.

2.0 Assessment

Our education system at all levels will leverage the power of technology to measure what matters and use assessment data for continuous improvement.

To meet this goal, we recommend the following actions:

2.1 Design, develop, and adopt assessments that give students, educators, and other stakeholders timely and actionable feedback about student learning to improve achievement and instructional practices.

2.2 Build the capacity of educators and educational institutions to use technology to improve assessment materials and processes for both formative and summative uses.

2.3 Conduct research and development that explore how gaming technology, simulations, collaboration environments, and virtual worlds can be used in assessments to engage and motivate learners and to assess complex skills and performances embedded in standards.

2.4 Revise practices, policies, and regulations to ensure privacy and information protection while enabling a model of assessment that includes ongoing student learning data gathering and sharing for continuous improvement.

3.0 Teaching

Professional educators will be supported individually and in teams by technology that connects them to data, content, resources, expertise, and learning experiences that enable and inspire more effective teaching for all learners.

To meet this goal, we recommend the following actions:

3.1 Design, develop, and adopt technology-based content, resources, and online learning communities that create opportunities for educators to collaborate for more effective teaching, inspire and attract new people into the profession, and encourage our best educators to continue teaching.

3.2 Provide pre-service and in-service educators with preparation and professional learning experiences powered by technology that close the gap between students' and educators' fluencies with technology and promote and enable technology use in ways that improve learning, assessment, and instructional practices.

3.3 Transform the preparation and professional learning of educators and education leaders by leveraging technology to create career-long personal learning networks within and across schools, pre-service preparation and in-service educational institutions, and professional organizations.

3.4 Use technology to provide access to the most effective teaching and learning resources, especially where they are not otherwise available, and to provide more options for all learners at all levels.

3.5 Develop a teaching force skilled in online instruction.

4.0 Infrastructure

All students and educators will have access to a comprehensive infrastructure for learning when and where they need it.

To meet this goal, we recommend the following actions:

4.1 Ensure that students and educators have adequate broadband access to the Internet and adequate wireless connectivity both inside and outside school.

4.2 Ensure that every student and educator has at least one Internet access device and software and resources for research, communication, multimedia content creation, and collaboration for use in and out of school.

4.3 Leverage open educational resources to promote innovative and creative opportunities for all learners and accelerate the development and adoption of new open technology-based learning tools and courses.

4.4 Build state and local education agency capacity for evolving an infrastructure for learning.

4.5 Support "meaningful use" of educational and information technology in states and districts by establishing definitions, goals, and metrics.

5.0 Productivity

Our education system at all levels will redesign processes and structures to take advantage of the power of technology to improve learning outcomes while making more efficient use of time, money, and staff.

To meet this goal, we recommend the following actions:

5.1 Develop and adopt a common definition of productivity in education and more relevant and meaningful measures of learning outcomes and costs.

5.2 Improve policies and use technology to manage costs including those for procurement.

5.3 Fund the development and use of interoperability standards for content, student learning data, and financial data to enable collecting, sharing, and analyzing data to improve decision making at all levels of our education system.

5.4 Rethink basic assumptions in our education system that inhibit leveraging technology to improve learning, starting with our current practice of organizing student and educator learning around seat time instead of the demonstration of competencies.

5.5 Design, implement, and evaluate technology-powered programs and interventions to ensure that students progress through our K–16 education system and emerge prepared for the workplace and citizenship.

Source: Office of Educational Technology (2010, pp. 10–12), *Transforming American Education: Learning Powered by Technology: National Education Technology Plan 2010, Executive Summary,* http://www.ed.gov/technology/netp-2010.

2 Teachers

The Magic Link Between Technology and Students

The magic link between the technology and the student is the teacher. If the teacher is dynamic and passionate about technology, the student will feel the "current."

Teachers are key to the implementation of technology in a classroom. The principal must enlist and enable teachers' leadership in all aspects of instruction as well as in the integration of technology into instruction.

Teachers as instructional leaders need the support of principals in this role. In schools that are traditional, bureaucratic institutions characterized by top-down leadership, teachers have limited leadership opportunities. The conditions that foster teacher leadership often do not exist. Teachers as instructional leaders flourish in collegial, collaborative settings. In these settings, teachers can engage in instructional improvement and instructional leadership (Glickman, Gordon, & Ross-Gordon, 2006).

INCENTIVES

School systems spend considerable resources on technology purchases as well as on the costs of maintaining and upgrading the technology. Districts also invest in technology training for teachers. These training experiences may provide teachers with the skills they need to use the technology, but teachers who have technology skills may not have the confidence or the know-how necessary to integrate technology into instruction.

Providing incentives for teachers to integrate technology into instruction is a common technique to encourage innovation. School districts, intermediate service units, professional associations, and other educator groups may offer stipends or grants for teachers to attend workshops or weeklong trainings that focus on developing lessons that incorporate technology. These incentive programs are often successful with the individuals who could be labeled early adopters (Rogers, 2003). These individuals are "open" to innovation and are prime targets for incentives. However, the incentive approach may not engage the remaining teachers in technology innovation.

A teacher-led professional development day may be the stimulus that will encourage teachers to integrate technology into their instruction. Corder, Marshall, Lineweaver, and McIntyre (2008) describe a teacher-led experience focused on developing lessons that integrate technology into existing curricula (p. 28).

In the experience, teachers were encouraged to work collaboratively in teams, select a project, and identify additional training needs. Using this information, a professional development day was scheduled. On the training day, teachers attended short sessions based on their training needs and then used the day to work on their projects. The teacher leaders who organized the session were available to provide assistance throughout the day. Groups met by curricular areas to share their experiences and ideas, and all teachers met at the end of the day to share their projects. The authors noted that few projects were completed, but the groups had plans for continuing the work. Evaluations of the day were mostly positive. Teachers, however, did not like being "required" to participate (Corder, Marshall, Lineweaver, & McIntyre, 2008).

TECHNOLOGY USE

The literature about teacher use of technology revealed the following finding: "A major focus of educational reforms in teacher preparation programs has been to develop a curriculum that prepares classroom teachers to incorporate technology into classroom learning" (Mayo, Kajs, & Tanguma, 2005, p. 3). For principals, this finding is a reminder to identify the level of teacher preparation for technology use as part of the new teacher interviewing process.

Williams and Kingham (2003) found "a lack of infusion of technology into the curriculum. . . . The veteran teachers . . . showed very little use of technology in the subject areas. . . . School districts may not be providing adequate staff development experiences to prepare veteran teachers to use technology in their classrooms" (para. 1).

In a study reported by Brown (2007), four of the six participants reported using technology more for administrative purposes than for instructional purposes. These uses included recording attendance and grades, submitting lesson plans, and checking email. Technology was described as "another subject." Technology was used as a means of increasing standardized test scores through emphasis on "drill and practice in math and reading" (p. 12).

In another example provided by Brown (2007),

> a teacher received an interactive whiteboard and digital projector at the beginning of the school year. She responded, "We never received formal training on our [interactive whiteboards]." She also indicated that no one had told them to turn off their projectors instead of just "muting" them because the bulb was still burning in the muted state. This could result in a short bulb life and needless increased expense for a school district. (p. 14)

Bauer and Kenton (2005) reported a study of 30 tech-savvy teachers. The teachers were "highly educated, skilled with technology, innovative, and adept at overcoming obstacles" (p. 519). However, "they did not integrate technology consistently as a teaching and learning tool because students did not have enough time at computers and teachers need additional planning time for technology lessons" (p. 519).

A West Virginia superintendent described a technology initiative in his district. "We've used the Palm [handhelds] to take the lead in the use of technology in West Virginia. We've set the stage for the 21st Century skills program in blending technology into everyday instructional classroom life" (Patton, 2006, p. 14):

> "I [the superintendent] made it an administrative goal and an expectation in their evaluation process," he says of his decision to purchase Palm handheld units. "We subtly pushed them along in order to get them more adept at using the Palm handheld on a day-to-day basis." (p. 10)
>
> His [superintendent's] persistence paid off. Just three years later he says each of the district's principals and roughly half of its 700 teachers now use Palm handhelds in a variety of ways. Principals rely on it to do everything from conducting teacher evaluations to sending important documents or messages to faculty and other administrators. Teachers use it for classroom management and to help deliver instruction. (pp. 10–11)

McPherson, Wizer, and Pierrel (2006) suggest teachers should "systematically collect evidence on the effects of their instruction on students, and the infusion of technology into that instruction" (p. 30). In the interest of technology use, teachers should identify "the value added by infusing technology into the unit of instruction" (p. 30).

GENERATIONAL SHIFT

During an interview, an administrator described the generational shift occurring in schools:

Most of us beyond a certain age are much more comfortable looking things up on pages rather than reading things and using the tools on a computer. It's just not as comfortable for us as it is for the younger ones. We've got a real shift coming in, between the generations of teachers, in how they're going to use technology, and it's not really being directed by anybody right now. It's morphing and changing as the younger teachers come in.

Higher education is doing a much better job of relying on it [technology], and kids learn it from each other at the college level. When they come into the classroom as teachers, they bring those skills with them and that comfort level. Until we get a majority of that generation of kids [who are the] teachers teaching, I think we will continue to struggle with the use of technology and the application of technology.

An assumption is that teachers who are "earlier in their careers" may be more adept with integration of technology into instruction than their more experienced peers. Based on interviews with administrators, their comments suggest that the assumption may be reality in some settings. Following are their comments:

That is one thing that I do find interesting with our younger teachers. They have a lot of enthusiasm; they like this technology piece.

To the newer teachers, it's not much of a problem because they embrace the technology.

Our experience has been that the younger the teachers are, the more readily they grasp technology. They like it and everybody knows that. But we really have had great resistance from our older teachers. We use the Teach for America teachers. They just embrace it and run with it, and other new teachers do that as well. The older teachers don't. We have a lot of fear of technology by the older, more established teachers.

You always have your early implementers—early adopters who are willing to try something new. With a lot of retirements, we have a lot younger staff who tend to be very comfortable with technology and who have had that experience as they've gone through college and in their own personal life.

They use technology a lot to communicate with friends. The other 50% are the 12-plus year educators and beyond who—technology is frightening, and it kind of takes over some of the control that we are used to having in our classroom, and we don't know how to let go of that control and let students utilize technology that we don't understand at all. We want student-centered learning, and we want student-centered classrooms, but giving over that control is very difficult and technology is sort of speeding up that transition. A lot of the more veteran teachers are not very comfortable with that. I become the forcing function [the driving force]: "OK, we're all going to try this little Ning project together and we're all going to post. I'm going to do a professional development session on just how to log in and how to become a member of this and show you where the questions are. Then, we're going to sit here together, and I'm going to give you 10 minutes to answer this question to give you some practice, so you can go back and answer the other questions on your own."

Teachers know that they have to drill down to those individual students, and they're not afraid of the data programs that can help them do that.

New teachers often need training on emailing. Don't respond in writing. . . . Don't respond in anger. You can get yourself in trouble fast. People are nastier when they don't have to talk to you face-to-face.

Veteran teachers may be reluctant to use technology. Another group of teachers who may pose challenges for administrators are difficult teachers. Comments by administrators included the following:

If they don't know about it—it's like the window just comes crashing down.

Usually, it's the people who are toward the end of their career, or they're people who just aren't interested in teaching and they're not there for the passion of it at all. They're there for a paycheck and because they didn't know what else to do—we still have people like that.

We've even had some difficult times getting some teachers to use projectors and their computers and PowerPoints, and you know virtually any textbook anymore that you buy is [linked to the use of these technology tools].

The older teachers, in my experience, have been . . . it's quite difficult. They don't want to give up their little annual unit on dinosaurs—whether it has anything to do with the central competencies or not. They really resist drilling down; they resist learning to use the programs; they resist having to put the data in. . . . I've had a lot of trouble with that. . . . If the principal doesn't make it happen, it won't happen. You just can't get it done if the principal isn't on the teachers to get that data in and then to pull it back up and to review it.

We have a challenge with faculty dragging their feet. They should use the online resources, not the old encyclopedia. We need to get these tools in kids' hands, but we have to bring the teachers along.

Each school setting is unique. The principal's challenge is to assess school needs and enlist the teachers in achieving the goals for the school. Incentives to stimulate technology use include money and time. Following are administrators' comments:

If they wanted the tools, they had to show up. We paid them as well.

The principals and the teachers always expected somebody else to put in the data—and frankly, there is nobody else. It's got to be the teachers, but in all fairness, it's important for the principals to make sure that the teachers have some time to do that. They've got to have some time to get it done. Once you have everything set up, it's really quite easy.

Often the best method of inspiring technology use is the influence of other teachers:

Just like when you put your SmartBoard—your first interactive board in the classroom and you have a teacher who just gets so excited about it, and other teachers are passing by and they say, "How come I don't have one of those?"

Technology use must be a clearly identified goal so that teachers know the use of technology is an expectation:

In our district, technology is one of our goals and our objectives. So it is an expectation and everyone accepts that.

You can train them to death. I trained mine to death, but they just never did it. It was not one of those things that rose to the top of their list of the to-dos for the day. . . . You must evaluate those teachers on those. They have to know that that's going to be part of their evaluation.

They're always telling me, "You don't need to teach them how to do this." What you do have to teach—you have to teach teachers that this is a possibility so that they assess their learning or their assignments or their projects or whatever and include these types of technologies in the final results or the final product.

One of the objectives is that they must produce a learning project where kids collaborate and communicate and use technology for learning. And they [students] will present those.

Principals must be attentive to teachers' technology use. The principal's task is to monitor goal attainment. Being visible and supportive of teacher efforts is critical to the successful attainment of goals:

The principal really has to check on a regular basis to make sure that the teacher is doing those things. If you do an electronic attendance, then that needs to be done every day. And if the principal will stay on it, it will be done.

The process of implementing technology use in teachers' skill repertoire is recursive:

You have to have them constantly coming back, getting with their peers, and talking about what's working, what isn't; you also have to have assignments. We bought a couple of books. We have assigned reading. We push people to read and think about and bring questions. We set up a Wiki on our server where they could do some of the discussion. The bottom line is, you must keep coming back. The thing of "the flash in the pan" will not work.

Roadblocks must be removed, or teachers lose interest and become frustrated:

It was so technical—the technology coordinator went on and on about safety and monitoring kids and making sure they're not going here or there and how they should know that our network is filtered and that he

checks it periodically to make sure to examine where the kids have been going. . . . There was a time when teachers just stopped using technology.

They'll quit doing it. They keep running into—it's called "access denied." . . . If they keep hitting that access denied, they quit using it because they don't have time.

Principals must recognize that technology is not "THE ANSWER":

It's not always appropriate, but I do think it can do wonderful things for us.

Technology is a set of tools that can assist teachers in their instructional efforts:

Having the tools, having the infrastructure, and having the time to train teachers, and then giving them time to plan . . . this is a whole new way of doing business . . . getting them to understand that technology isn't the answer. They're still going to have to get down and dirty with those kids to teach them how to read.

The principals' objective is to move teachers to "yes." The following administrator's remark reflects getting to "yes":

They learned tons, and toward the end of the day, they were starting to come around going, "This could really work; this could really help."

An example of a change in instructional practices is provided by an experienced administrator:

This grant has an iTouch for every single second grader. It had to be written for a classroom—I have some really young second-grade teachers, and they're very savvy with technology; that's why we chose that. Plus, we had some data that could show some real significant need of second grade as far as reading comprehension and vocabulary fluency. Those kids will have their own little earphones. Each classroom will have their download cart with the computer and the printer and a document camera

on it. They will practice their vocabulary, they will practice their fluency, and that feedback will be instantaneous.

The better teachers know how to keep the kids' attention and how to keep them engaged regardless. A really good teacher can keep the kids' interest—can set the stage when a child wants to learn—regardless of the tools that they may use. They know how to do that. And the bad teachers don't know how to do it. How the good teachers are going to use the technology in the classroom—you know there are ways to do it. And there are beginning to be programs that come out. You know, have kids use their cell phones to do projects.

ACTION AGENDA

- Use Figure 2.1 to identify teachers' use of technology.
- Follow the principal's exploration agenda: Explore the technology resources using the 15-minute-a-day approach.

Resources

Teacher's Use of Technology

Principal's Exploration Agenda

TEACHER'S USE OF TECHNOLOGY

Figure 2.1 Teacher's Use of Technology

Teacher's Name	Years of Teaching Experience	Stage of Technology Use	Tools Used

PRINCIPAL'S EXPLORATION AGENDA

Use the 15-minute-a-day approach to explore the vast resources related to technology. The following sites are places to begin the exploration:

Websites

- AOL for Kids: This site provides a collection of educator-reviewed online resources selected for K–2 students:

  http://kids.aol.com/KOL/2/HomeworkHelp/Archive/homework-help-jr

- Discovery Education: This site offers classroom resources including free lesson plans written by teachers for teachers:

  http://school.discoveryeducation.com/lessonplans

- Disney: This website offers suggestions to parents for child safety on the Internet:

  http://www.disney.go.com/surfswell

- Education World: This site offers resources for teachers from lesson plans to professional development opportunities:

  http://www.educationworld.com

- Glogster: This website provides a place to share creations such as posters, art, and scrapbooks:

  http://www.glogster.com

- Moodle: This site offers a course-management system that allows educators to create course sites for students:

  http://moodle.org

- NEA Academy: This site provides professional development, classroom tools, and a database that contains preselected education websites and lesson plans:

  http://sites.nea.org/academy/index.htmlx

- Search Engines: This website offers a list of search engines for Internet searches:

  http://www.searchengines.com

- Technologies for Teaching: San Diego State University offers a web-based course designed to help you become comfortable with technology:

  http://edweb.sdsu.edu/courses/edtec470/s10/4/index.htm

- 21st Century Literacies: This site focuses on 21st Century literacies including information, visual, cultural, and media skills:

  http://www.kn.pacbell.com/wired/21stcent

- Virtual Worlds and Kids: Mapping the Risks: The Federal Trade Commission offers advice for parents on protecting their children from virtual worlds:

  http://www.ftc.gov/bcp/edu/pubs/consumer/alerts/alt038.shtm

Software

- Evernote: Once downloaded, this software allows you to take notes and capture snippets from the web:

  http://www.evernote.com

- HyperStudio: This site offers educators licenses and discounted software for student tools to create exciting combinations of student media:

  http://www.mackiev.com/hyperstudio

- Inspiration: This software includes visual-thinking tools:

  http://www.inspiration.com

- iTunes U: This site allows educators to search for educational content for students:

  http://www.apple.com/education/itunes-u

- Jing: This free or low-cost software allows students and educators to create short voice-over screen captures:

  http://www.techsmith.com

- Renaissance Learning: This site provides advanced technology resources for educators:

  http://www.renlearn.com/neo/NEO2/default.aspx

- YouTube: This site holds a wealth of educational videos as well as provides a place for students to share their video creations:

  http://www.youtube.com

3 The Technology Leadership Team

Technology specialists and the technology leadership team are the focus of this chapter. Each school may have a different configuration in relation to the technology specialist and the technology leadership team. In some settings, these positions may be embedded in the curriculum or instruction department of a school.

Technology specialists and the technology team are essential partners in school technology leadership. The emphasis throughout the chapter is on the technology specialist's role and on the technology leadership team's contributions to technology leadership in the school. Considerations for the principal's work are presented throughout the chapter.

THE TECHNOLOGY SPECIALIST

A principal who leverages the talent, skills, and possibilities of the technology specialist is attentive to the following aspects of this individual's role in the school:

- Is the technology specialist an expert in (a) technology, (b) curriculum and instruction, or (c) both technology and curriculum and instruction?
- What qualifications does the technology specialist have?
- What qualifications do you seek in a technology specialist?
- Is the work of the technology specialist directly linked to student achievement?
- How closely is the technology specialist aligned with the curriculum specialists in the school?
- How is the technology specialist positioned in the school setting?
- How is the technology specialist perceived by the teachers?

- How is the work of the technology specialist apportioned?
- How prominent is technology integration in the curriculum of the school?

These considerations are the basis for the following description of the technology specialist's role. In the literature concerning technology, there are many different titles for this individual (see Figure 3.1).

Figure 3.1 Technology Titles

Technology Titles	
<ul><li>Computer specialist</li><li>Educational technologist</li><li>Instructional technologist</li><li>Instructional technology coordinator</li><li>Instructional technology specialist</li><li>Integration facilitator</li><li>Integration specialist</li></ul>	<ul><li>Media specialist</li><li>Technology coordinator</li><li>Technology facilitator</li><li>Technology integration specialist</li><li>Technology leader</li><li>Technology specialist</li><li>Technology support specialist</li></ul>

Qualifications

One measure of qualification in an educational setting is certification. "The benefits of certification include a sense of great achievement; increased self-confidence; professional growth; and maintenance of current targeted skills needed to install, configure, service, and maintain emerging technology" (Wright & Lesisko, 2007, p. 9). Wright and Lesisko found certification credentials offered by a state education agency or professional certification program for instructional technology leaders existed in 19 states. Technology leaders may have vendor certifications offered through manufacturers such as Microsoft, Cisco, and Novell: "Vendor certification is considered by corporate employers as actual proof of ability and skill" (Wright & Lesisko, p. 8). Computer certifications may be obtained through community colleges and technical schools in areas such as networking and database and project management (Davis, 2008).

Technology leaders may have teaching certificates. In a school setting, the technology leader may need skill in technology as well as in curriculum and instruction. The role has evolved as computers and technology have proliferated.

The challenge in a school and a school district is the division of tasks and the expectations of technology leaders. One division of tasks calls for one team of individuals to maintain the technology and another team of individuals to foster integration of technology into instruction. This division calls for the identification of two types of specialists.

Place and Lesisko (2005) suggest the title of *technology coordinator* for the individual who is not professionally certified. The technology coordinator's focus is on "installation, troubleshooting, maintenance, and support of technology resources" (p. 4):

We had remote access to every computer. It saved a lot of time and travel. . . . We separated it out: We had one person in charge of some of our student applications, like the Renaissance—you know, the reading and the math programs. We had another person in charge of our email and student information system [and] another person in charge of our networking and our routers and our wireless.

The *director of instructional technology* holds a professional technology certificate issued by a state department of education (Lesisko, 2004). This individual works to enhance the teaching, learning, and instruction process through the integration of technology, as appropriate, into the curricular areas.

Wright and Lesisko (2007) recommend two positions. A *director of education technology* "should be certified and have a background in education and be well educated in leadership, educational innovation, and curriculum development. A second area of knowledge and skill should include a background in information management, networking, Internet applications, infrastructure, technology support, and systems security" (p. 13). A second professional, the *network administrator,* "should have a graduate background in information technology or related field as well as certification by a national vendor . . . [and] have the responsibility of system maintenance and serve as the in-house consultant for all systems and be involved in all large-scale software and hardware purchases" (p. 13).

In a school setting, the director of instructional technology or the director of education technology would have the qualifications suggested in Figure 3.2.

Figure 3.2   Qualifications

Qualifications for Director of Instructional Technology

Knowledge Base

- Curriculum and instruction
- Theory of instructional technologies
- Emerging technologies
- Instructional software

(Continued)

Figure 3.2 (Continued)

Leadership Skills

- Interpersonal skills
- Communication skills
- Ability to establish a vision for instructional technology
- Change-agent skills
- Motivation skills
- Problem-solving skills
- Service orientation

Technical Skills

- Experience with hardware and software
- Experience with equipment maintenance
- Experience in management of network infrastructure
- Experience in inventory oversight
- Experience with network security

Source: Bushweller (1996); Frazier (2003); Lesisko (2005); Place and Lesisko (2005).

It's pretty rare to find a technology coordinator or director who has both sets of skills. "I want to do the infrastructure. I don't want to do the data. . . . I will build you a system that will power your school, but that's what I do . . ." Do you go with someone who keeps your network working and expanding, or do you go with someone who knows how to use the technology skills—the 21st Century skills—in the classroom and helps teachers integrate that into the classroom. It's almost like you've got two different characteristics going on. I always compare technology in school districts to a car and mechanics: You need someone to keep that car running. You need a very good mechanic who can go in there and do the maintenance and can diagnose the problem and keep it running. But then, you also need a driver—an expert driver—who can drive that vehicle and get it to where it's going. And sometimes, you're lucky enough to have one person who can do both.

Technology person—I never have had a curriculum-type person who's also technology . . . more of a techie. I ran all technology purchases through my technology director. She had final approval. If she didn't approve it, we didn't buy it. . . . They're responsible for finding you the best deal, for ensuring that your equipment works [and] that you've got hardware and software in place.

I was not only a network administrator and a technologist, but I really knew how to incorporate it and get the teachers excited about it. You can't just have a network administrator who works with it behind the scenes and just handles the network. You have to have someone who also knows the educational part about it and how we get our teachers excited—bringing in those tools and, then, not just handing them a tool but . . . saying, "OK, let me help you integrate this into your lesson plans. Let me help you bring this in." And if you don't have an administrator who supports all this, it's not going to make a difference at all.

Academic degrees, such as the bachelor's and master's degrees, are important qualifications in a school setting. Vendor certifications suggest additional qualifications in technology preparation. "Experiences working with Macintosh and PC platforms should be documented by applicants. Experience working with networks should be evident in an individual's experiences. Knowledge of internet and intranet technologies, multimedia systems, instructional design and assessments, and telecommunications systems are other desirable qualifications for technology leaders" (Place & Lesisko, 2005, pp. 13, 15). "What is clearly missing from the background of technologists is any formal or informal preparation for supporting curriculum and instruction in the schools. What these individuals lack is the ability to work with teachers and help them integrate technology into ongoing classroom activities" (Wright & Lesisko, 2007, p. 11).

The tech director was our band person, believe it or not. He's always been very savvy with technology and with computers. First of all, he became half-time band, half-time technology. We had some other band people besides him, and then we got into this money crunch, and of course, we couldn't support all of our music people at that point, and so we made him into our tech director—it was kind of by default.

She almost had an electrical engineering degree, so she did a lot of wiring herself, a lot of repair. . . . She had a basic user's kind of certificate. She had CISCO, and I think maybe she did have Microsoft.

There are two of them. They came out of the classroom, and they are much better with teachers. But they are also younger.

I try to learn as much as I can. I have an instructional coach who is traditionally, purely instructional, but she also is trying to learn a lot about technology. I am blessed to have an ROTC leader who is a retired [information technology] designer, so he's taking the lead on some of our building technology. He is the person who I go to a lot. So I have this computer guy in the building. If you don't have that—I don't know how other people are functioning.

We have a district technology center, but really, we have 11,000 students in the district, over 1,500 employees, and we have about 80 of them in one high school who are 1-to-1 laptops right now. So our resources are really spread too thin there. Our district technology center has a director whose background is business from about 20 years ago; he tries to stay apprised of technology. We have a couple of really smart guys who work there purchasing technology, but aside from purchasing, setting it up, and imaging the computers, there is not a lot of training that goes on.

THE TECHNOLOGY LEADERSHIP TEAM

Each school varies in the number of individuals who make up the technology leadership team. A first step for the principal is to identify the team members. A second step is to identify the strengths of each member of the technology leadership team.

A principal may be new to a school and may inherit the technology leadership team. In this case, the principal's task is to get to know these individuals. A principal who has been in the same school for a number of years may be comfortable with the technology leadership team. In this case, the school, the principal, and the technology leadership team have grown together through the ever-expanding opportunities made possible by new technologies. The principal of this school may need to examine the status of the technology leadership team and how it has grown and changed in recent years.

Identify the Team

The technology leadership team may include the principal, technology specialist, curriculum director, instructional facilitator, librarian, media specialist, teachers, and students, as well as the stakeholders indicated in Figure 3.3. The size of the school will help determine the size of the team. The titles of the individuals who are members of the leadership team vary from school to school. The essential feature of the team is that all the stakeholders in technology integration into instruction are represented on the team (see Figure 3.3).

The role of the technology leadership team is to

- Establish policies
- Identify technology that can be integrated into instruction
- Identify professional development needs
- Suggest hardware and software purchases
- Advocate for technology integration into instruction

An effective team is one that is able to clearly articulate the needs of the school and then problem solve to meet the needs. Decisions made by a

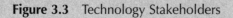

Figure 3.3 Technology Stakeholders

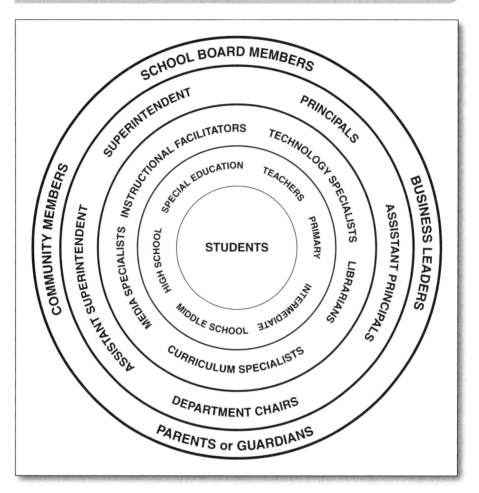

technology leadership team allow consensus to be built and do not require the principal or the technology specialist to stand as the sole decision maker.

Principals are at different stages of involvement in technology use in the school. Principals who are passionate about technology applications may have daily engagement in this aspect of the school:

Those people [the tech savvy] can see the possibility, so they have to teach me. And they have; they're constantly feeding me articles. They want the best for their kids. They see me as somebody who can help them get stuff for their kids.

Principals who have limited interest in technology applications in instruction may delegate this aspect of the school's program to an assistant or may simply trust the technology leadership team with complete autonomy in their work:

The reason that I am doing the technology committee is because we were not moving forward. I really did not think that was my job, but it is. I don't have a vote on that committee—or at least I set it up that way—and I'm strictly the facilitator.

The principal's involvement in technology can be displayed along a continuum, such as the one in Figure 3.4.

Figure 3.4 Principal's Involvement

Continuum of Principal's Involvement With Technology Use in the School

Infrequent Involvement   *Daily Involvement*

← — — — — — — — — — — — — — — — →

Infrequent Engagement With   Daily Engagement With
Technology and Technology   Technology and Technology
Leadership Team   Leadership Team

Conversations

The principal must schedule time for getting to know the technology leadership team members. The principal should approach this process guided by questions designed to elicit the strengths of each individual and to discover how each individual apportions work time. These questions need to be presented in a nonthreatening manner. The principal is seeking to understand and clarify this valuable area of work in the school. The product of these conversations will be a portrait of the strengths and qualifications of the technology leadership team members. From this information, the principal will be able to speak knowledgeably about the work of the team.

As part of the conversations, the principal will want to determine the aspects of the work individuals take the greatest pride in—their greatest accomplishments. The principal can share these successes with the various stakeholders of the school. These discussions will strengthen the principal's ability to advocate for the importance of technology in the school and showcase these accomplishments.

The conversations with the team members will allow the principal to identify the needs of the team based on the experiences of the individuals who work with technology each day.

The time invested in these conversations has benefits for the entire school community. Through the conversations, the technology leadership team members are acknowledged for their efforts. Their work is seen as valuable when it is given the focused attention of the principal. By sponsoring this discussion, the principal becomes more aware of the possibilities of technology use and integration into the curriculum and can serve as a well-informed spokesperson. Through these communications, the principal displays support for technology use and serves as a technology leader. The principal's display of interest and commitment to technology use elevates the importance of technology in the school.

Location

Schools as bureaucratic organizations have features that can elevate or bury individuals, positions, programs, and departments. Consider the issue of space. As student populations exceed the capacity envisioned when buildings were constructed, which individuals, positions, or programs are displaced by the crush of enrollment? Those who have inhabited schools for any amount of time can roll their eyes and recall which programs and personnel are relocated to airless cubicles that challenge the integrity of the academic programs.

The simple question is, Where are the technology leadership team members located in the school? Is their space close to the core activity of the school—the teaching and learning? Are teachers able to access these individuals easily? Are the technology leaders and curriculum leaders in close proximity? Are curriculum leaders essential members of the technology leadership team?

Placement conveys a clear message to individuals inside and outside of the school. If a goal is to increase the use of technology, to better integrate technology into instruction, or to prepare for a more technology-rich curriculum, the principal should examine the location of the technology leadership team in the school:

I had my director of technology on my cabinet—the Superintendent's Cabinet. . . . She reported directly to me. The technology person needs to be in the upper echelon because everything in your district is linked through technology.

The article "More Than a Techie" (Technology & Learning, 2008) supports this superintendent's approach: "Tomorrow's CIO/CTO—whether in industry or education—will be less of a techie and more of a business or education leader" (p. 1). In education, this will require "the CTO to serve as a cabinet member and delegate IT implementation to a highly qualified technology expert" (p. 2).

ACTION AGENDA

- Identify the role of the technology specialist in the school.
- Identify the technology leadership team members.
- Identify the stakeholders in technology integration in the school.
- Identify your location on the "Continuum of Principal's Involvement With Technology Use in the School" (see Figure 3.4).
- Follow the principal's exploration agenda: Explore the technology resources using the 15-minute-a-day approach.

Resources

Technology Specialist in the School

Principal's Exploration Agenda

TECHNOLOGY SPECIALIST IN THE SCHOOL

Use the technology specialist checklist to examine the placement of this individual in the school.

Figure 3.5   The Technology Specialist

The technology specialist is

☐ An expert in technology
☐ An expert in curriculum and instruction
☐ An expert in both technology and curriculum and instruction

Is the work of the technology specialist directly linked to student achievement?

☐ Yes   ☐ No

How closely aligned are the technology specialist and the Curriculum Department?

☐ Not closely aligned   ☐ Somewhat aligned   ☐ Closely aligned

How is the technology specialist positioned in the hierarchy of the school?

☐ Far removed from   ☐ In the middle of the   ☐ Close to the
   the principal   school hierarchy   principal

PRINCIPAL'S EXPLORATION AGENDA

Use the 15-minute-a-day approach to explore the following resource:

- The Microsoft Digital Literacy website may be useful in encouraging emerging technology leaders in the school:

  http://www.microsoft.com/About/CorporateCitizenship/Citizenship/giving/programs/UP/digitalliteracy/eng/Curriculum.mspx

Part II
Core Issues

4 Professional Development

The Teacher-to-Teacher Approach

Teachers are on the frontline of technology use. Students may come to school with technology skills that exceed those of the teacher. Other students, who come to school with limited technology skills, must depend on teachers to provide technology instruction as well as subject-area instruction. This is a 21st Century case of the "haves" and "have-nots," or the digital divide, in schools.

There appears to be a comparable case of "haves" and "have-nots" among teachers. For principals, teachers' reluctance to use technology is a concern. Principals must provide the professional development teachers need. As newly adopted curriculum materials come with an increasing array of supplemental technology resources, teachers must embrace and use these companion technology tools. Textbooks come with a variety of resources to enrich student learning activities. Textbooks also come with a variety of resources to support instruction and assessment. Teachers need the skills and time to plan how to integrate these resources into their instructional activities as well as the ability to use the supplemental materials available to them.

Teachers approach technology as they approach other innovations. Teachers are at various stages of adoption as described in Rogers' (2003) *Diffusion of Innovations.*

According to one administrator,

 It depends. Some people absolutely throw themselves into it. . . . Well, it's totally Rogers. You know. There's the pioneers and then . . . We have a lot of early adopters, but you still have some that . . . you have to push and shove.

The Concerns Based Adoption Model (CBAM) provides guidance to principals as they assist teachers in making changes in their instructional practices. CBAM includes a framework for the identification of teachers' readiness to make changes in their teaching practices. It is a framework that has been used successfully for many years.

STAGES OF CONCERN

Figure 4.1 Stages of Concern About Technology Use

STAGES OF CONCERN ABOUT TECHNOLOGY USE

(CBAM: Concerns Based Adoption Model)

In facilitating change, you need to know what concerns individuals have about technology use, especially their most intense concerns. These concerns will have a powerful influence on the implementation of change and how and if they use technology. CBAM offers several ways to identify these concerns. As a change agent, you can use this model to identify concerns, interpret them, and then act on them.

Stages	Description	Stages to Guide Change
Awareness	• May or may not know about technology • May or may not be ready to use technology	❑ Involve teachers in discussions and decisions ❑ Share enough information to stir interest, but not to overwhelm ❑ Provide open environment where all questions are allowed and lack of awareness is accepted ❑ Minimize gossip and inaccurate sharing of information
Informational	• Wants to learn more about the technology • Curious how technology can be used with students	❑ Share information through all forms of media ❑ Find those that are using the technology on- and off-site and have them share what they are doing ❑ Help teachers see how technology relates to their teaching practices ❑ Be enthusiastic about all who are using technology
Personal	• Has concerns about proficiency level	❑ Know these concerns are common and legitimize existence of concerns

Stages	Description	Stages to Guide Change
	• Does not want to look foolish at a workshop	❏ Connect teachers with similar concerns and those who will be supportive ❏ Share how technology can be used in small attainable steps
Management	• Wants practical suggestions on how to use technology for specific purposes • Needs help with specific problems	❏ Explain components of technology and share "how-tos" ❏ Demonstrate practical solutions to logistical problems ❏ Help teachers create a timeline or plan on how to use technology for immediate concerns
Consequence	• Uses technology but not sure how to use with students or what activities are out there that use technology	❏ Provide opportunities to attend conferences or visit other teachers using technology with students ❏ Share lessons involving technology and post student work ❏ Give these people positive feedback and access to resources
Collaborative	• Would like to share lessons with other teachers • Offers technical support to others	❏ Provide opportunities to develop their skills ❏ Provide common planning time for these teachers ❏ Look for opportunities for these teachers to team on projects ❏ Use these teachers as mentors or coaches
Refocusing	• Looks for ways to improve program • Serves on technology committee • Thinks "outside the box"	❏ Encourage these teachers to research and test new ideas and technologies ❏ Provide access to all resources so they can refine their ideas and put them into practice ❏ Allow these teachers to take risks

The principal must visit with each teacher to assess the teacher's knowledge and use of technology. This information forms the basis for planning professional development activities for teachers. Professional development must be designed to meet the teachers' needs at their various stages of technology use. The professional development events must be planned to accommodate the teachers' "readiness to learn." For some teachers, the acquisition of technology skills and know-how will be swift and painless. For other teachers, the learning process will be slow and incremental. Technology skills acquisition may require many repetitions of instruction and repeated opportunities to practice new skills.

One administrator described a grant-funded project that included successive follow-ups, assignments, and presentations of lessons:

We have a project going on right now, and it's all about integrating technology into the classroom. It is heavy-duty staff development. First of all, we gave them all the little "tools" and let them play with them. Then we brought them in—two times thus far. One time was for an all-day Saturday—and if you want to think I was popular on that day, think again. . . . But anyway, if they wanted the tools, they had to show up, and of course, we paid them as well for that day. They learned tons, and toward the end of the day, they were starting to say, "This could really work; this could really help." Then we had a follow-up. After we had the all-day follow-up, then we had an evening thing where we brought them in, fed them, and we went again. We talked about what's working, where are your problems, tell us some of your successes, tell us some of your concerns, [and] tell us where you're just absolutely crashing. We had a trainer who we had contracted come back and help them walk through it. They're coming back again and we will have another all-day thing, and then, we'll have another evening thing where we will present our projects. We will also take some of these projects to [an] Education Technology Association meeting.

Another professional development activity was described by a high school principal who models the use of the technology tools for teachers:

What I'm trying to do is get teachers comfortable with using technology for communication and collaboration. . . . Where face-to-face used to be the mode, lots of kids are going to Facebook and social networking sites. Teachers can't teach 21st Century skills using technological sources and sites unless they have the skill and the practice themselves.

I post questions; we have dialogue; I post videos. So if they have their kids do something on a Wiki site or they build something interactive for their students to use, they're not doing it cold. They have gone through the kind of metacognitive process of, How does this assist my own learning, so I can teach kids how it can assist their learning? We're expecting a lot of teachers who have been trained in very traditional methods of instructional delivery. They have never utilized this kind of technology. They're not comfortable with it. They may not have access to it, and they don't understand it.

TEACHER TO TEACHER

Based on Rogers' studies, the teachers of technology use in instructional settings should be teachers. Teachers learn from teachers. The approach to professional development should be as follows:

- Identify the teachers' skills and knowledge of technology
- Plan activities that match the skill and knowledge level of the teachers
- Schedule and deliver the activities
- Plan to repeat activities until teachers have mastered the skills
- Allow teachers to practice the skills and demonstrate the use of the technology
- Provide time for skill practice
- Feature teachers as the facilitators of the sessions to emphasize the teacher-to-teacher model of diffusion of innovations
- Provide time and resources to allow the sessions to be successful and to demonstrate the value placed on the activities
- Monitor and record the successes and progress that is made as a result of the professional development activities

The professional development model (Figure 4.2) is an illustration of this approach.

PROFESSIONAL DEVELOPMENT AGENDA

One goal of professional development should be digital literacy for all teachers. Teachers need to be digitally literate in order to "help students develop skills and knowledge that they will need to succeed in the 21st century workplace, where technology dominates" (Franek, 2005–2006, p. 41).

Professional development must be offered concerning cyberbullying. "Training also helps staff understand the parameters of acceptable and unacceptable conduct and respond to incidents either witnessed or brought to their attention" (MacFarlane, 2007, p. 3). Staff need to know who to notify and the policies and procedures of the school district, as well as local, state, and federal laws. This information needs to be reviewed annually with all

Figure 4.2 Professional Development Model

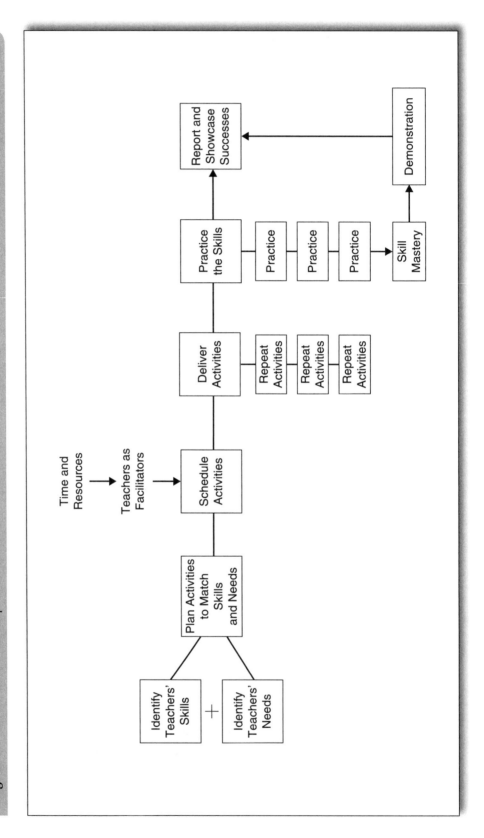

staff. As technology changes, safety and use concerns change as well. In response, policies, procedures, and laws must adapt to the changes. The annual updates are an essential part of the professional development cycle.

Staff members need professional development on the incidence of cyberbullying. This update includes "how and where most cyberbullying occurs, how to recognize the behavior, its damaging effect (social, behavioral, and academic), and how to prevent and respond to it" (Feinberg & Robey, 2008, p. 12).

The mention of professional development may elicit resistance. For instance, as a professional, do you want to be told you need professional development? Consider the professional development activities you have experienced during your career. How would you rate those events? Based on these experiences, resistance to professional development may be expected. An administrator made the following comments:

It is all dependent on how good the professional developers are. The thing that I discovered was that not all are created equal. If you are lucky enough to have great professional developers, you get great training. They're the ones who kind of show you the way, where the types of skills are that you need.

NEED BASED

Professional development must be designed to meet the identified needs. Activities must be aligned with the knowledge and skills of the individuals who will be the participants. Administrators offered the following comments:

Once you have an awareness of where you want to take the school, you kind of seek out the types of training that you want. You have to have that awareness and especially with technology. For someone my age, it's not intuitive to me, and so I have to learn it and somebody really has to show me. . . . You know—your kids really need this. Or your teachers need to know how to do this. And after I developed that awareness, it's so easy to find the PD that I need.

Looking at professional development—we have amazing teachers out there—they've been bombarded by this new technology, the 21st Century skills, and wait a minute—how do I incorporate these into my lesson plans? You do that through assessing the teachers and then bringing in the professional development that we need.

ADMINISTRATOR INVOLVEMENT

One reason professional development activities in schools are not successful is the absence of administrators from the activities. Change or innovation relies on administrative involvement, support, and leadership.

One administrator, describing an elementary professional development activity, noted she requires participation from "all the instructors. I even bring the special education director in."

We kind of expect that all educators know how to use technology, what is appropriate and what is inappropriate. We don't do a good job of training them. The administrators that I have talked to who are comfortable with technology, it seems like we're all self-taught. So very few of us have gone to classes. Very few of us have had formal training. We just have had to learn it to keep up with our profession. And some of us have and some of us have not. The skill level is just all over the board, and we need to address that better than we're addressing it.

ACTION AGENDA

- Use the teacher-to-teacher approach to professional development.
- Follow the professional development model.

5 Cybersafety Leadership

Guarding the Borders

In the spirit of "add a role," principals have assumed the role of school safety expert. The role is a natural response to the challenging issues that occur in school settings. Issues such as school violence, student harassment, and bullying have precipitated this shift in focus. The emphasis on student behavior has adjusted to accommodate the changing school environment.

At the school's frontier, the issue du jour has become the opportunities and challenges provided by technology. A major challenge, cybersafety is a prominent concern for principals, teachers, students, parents, and communities.

Principals are expected to assume responsibility and leadership for technology. However, the parameters of the responsibility must be defined. The ambiguous aspects of the boundaries of technology have become apparent to school leaders. Questions that focus the principals' concerns are presented in Figure 5.1.

Figure 5.1 Boundaries of Technology Focus Questions

Boundaries
- What are the boundaries of the school's involvement in student activities related to technology?
- What are the risks?
- What are the key concerns for principals?
- What guidelines related to technology use should be in place?
- What instruction concerning cybersafety should be provided for students?
- What professional development activities should be available to teachers and staff?
- What instruction concerning cybersafety should be offered to families?

BOUNDARIES

The challenges that result from the availability of technology "center on the struggle to provide a safe educational setting when the environment is no longer limited to the physical structure of the building" (MacFarlane, 2007, p. 1). The U.S. Supreme Court decision in *Tinker v. Des Moines Independent Community School District* (1969) introduced the legal principle associated with "the schoolhouse gate." This principle is linked to cyberbullying in that it places limits on the authority school leaders can exercise in cyberbullying situations. "Tinker provides that a school may only restrict student speech that causes a substantial and material disruption of school activities because students do not shed their constitutional rights, including their rights to free speech, at the schoolhouse gate" (Taylor, 2008, p. 61).

Schools "are restricted from taking disciplinary action against cyberbullies if the incidents take place outside of the school" (Sutton, 2009, p. 40). According to Sutton, "Only seven states have passed laws pertaining to cyberbullying" (p. 40).

The "blurring" of the "line between work and home" is another aspect of the "less distinct" boundaries due to the expansion of technology (Ashmore & Herman, 2006). The use of the Internet, email, Facebook, Twitter, and blogs by teachers, staff, and students are examples of the pervious school-home boundaries.

RISKS AND CHALLENGES

The threats to student and school safety appear to be a moving target for school leaders and parents. Wolinsky (2008) describes Internet safety issues such as pornography and bullying. Administrators' comments on the risks and challenges include the following:

The locker room absolutely scares me to death . . . taking a cell phone or an iTouch or something and taking little pictures here and there. . . . We've had kids who have snuck a phone into a chemistry class, and they've taken a picture of the test and then sent it to their buddies, you know, on the sly. . . . Facebook—it's instantaneous . . . and it's become meaner. You know, as time goes on, they just keep upping the ante.

With the cyberbullying and the use of cell phones in schools—it's just a nightmare trying to establish any type of control over the use of cell phones. I think most districts have just kind of given up.

The sex thing and the bullying is just—it's horrible. The impact that it's having on kids is just remarkable because, in our day and age, kids could pass a note around and it was a very limited audience. . . . Now, it's spread throughout the whole town, throughout the whole community—really, throughout the whole country almost immediately. For vulnerable kids, you know they could have moved to another district and been OK, but now that follows these kids around.

———————————

FILTERING OR NOT?

Blocking pornography through filtering was a first step in the effort to create a safe environment for students. Overblocking the content through filtering became the downside of this effort. Protecting the privacy of students and protecting students from predators became additional safety concerns.

Administrators' experiences with filtering are reflected in the following comments:

I've decided that most technology directors in schools are control freaks and they love filtering. They love putting controls on your network. And it's a constant battle with them. I am constantly duking it out; I just had a major battle getting him to open up YouTube for the teachers. There are incredible lessons on YouTube.

I used to bring him in for a new teacher program to talk about our district's technology. It was so technical: He went on and on about safety and monitoring kids and making sure they're not going here or there and how they should know that our network is filtered. . . . Our teachers—there was a time when they just stopped using technology. They couldn't get there.

I couldn't figure out why this one site was—I couldn't get there. And I just couldn't see what was causing it to stop, and finally figured out that there was one page that had the word game *in it and it stopped it. The whole thing was stopped.*

This is what is happening to teachers day in and day out. . . . They have 20 to 25 kids sitting there. The teacher's telling them to go to abc, you know, .com or .org or whatever, and then they're getting their access denied. We want kids to go out there and problem solve, gather information, bring it back, wrestle with the information, use it in some constructive way. But yet you want us to tell them the sites that they can go to. . . . That's not real life.

They need to educate themselves on how to utilize the tools of the World Wide Web. They may find their first link, and on there, they find it blocked. Well, it's not a good educational resource or else it would not be blocked. Instead, work with your technology department with creating catalogs. Then, they're not being blocked. You've created a good educational catalog. Kids aren't being exposed to things they're not supposed to be exposed to, and the teachers have the resources that they need.

Now, I realize that we need to filter because of E-rate and so on. But you know, E-rate isn't nearly so constraining; I finally figured that out. It's mainly the sexual piece. Even the violence isn't so much there. Sexual exploitation is the main piece of that federal law.

Cyberbullying is another safety concern. Inappropriate and rude behavior linked to social networking sites contributes to incivility (Kornblum, 2007). The threats and challenges change constantly as the prevalence and possibilities of technology transform students' lives, schools, and society. The school leader's challenge is to keep pace with these changes.

Acceptable Use

Principals must be knowledgeable about students' rights and employees' rights. Free speech is a key factor in use of the Internet, blogs, chat rooms, and cyberbullying. Schools must have clear acceptable use policies to provide the framework for students, parents, and teachers. The policies must be reviewed annually to verify that they are compatible with contemporary technology and school practices. A "Technology Use Guidelines" survey is provided in the resources. The policies and practices are district concerns as well as school-level concerns.

Principals must ensure that teachers and staff are provided with professional development related to emerging technologies and district policies. One administrator described the following process:

Every year, I do a compliance training and I outline the things that are acceptable, unacceptable, and then I outline the mandatory policy briefs that all staff have to sign off on that they have been informed about. I will inform them about their legal expectation of privacy being very low on [when using] district technology. I will inform them about sexual harassment, about bullying, about mandated reporting of child abuse and neglect—all of the policy training that has to happen. And then, a big part of what I talk about is, be careful who you friend on Facebook, be careful what photos you post, those kinds of things.

Students and parents also sign the acceptable use policies as a condition of using the Internet, district resources, and acquiring laptops. See the "Principal's Exploration Agenda" for links to samples of acceptable use policies (AUP).

CYBERSAFETY LEADERSHIP

Through national media attention, the negative aspects of technology use have become common knowledge. These reports have fueled fear, anxiety, and skepticism about technology in the schools. However, the prevalence of misuse and abuse is limited. For this reason, principals must direct efforts to "what schools should do best: anticipate, prepare, and educate" (Sutton, 2009, p. 40).

The principal must provide leadership in establishing the cybersafety plan for the school. The focus of cybersafety leadership is on digital citizenship education, civility education, parent education, and teacher education (see Figure 5.2).

Figure 5.2 Cybersafety Leadership

Cybersafety Leadership
- Digital citizenship education
- Civility education
- Parent education
- Teacher education

Digital Citizenship Education

The first task is to promote digital citizenship education for all who use the school's technology tools. Ribble and Bailey's (2004) "list of misuse and abuse includes hacking into school servers, using email to intimidate or threaten students, illegally downloading music, plagiarizing information from the Internet, using cellular phones during class time, accessing pornographic websites, and playing video games during class" (p. 1). Their suggestion for addressing these issues is a digital citizenship audit. Using the findings of the audit, they recommend creating a digital citizenship program that addresses appropriate technology behavior (Ribble & Bailey). See the resource "Principal's Exploration Agenda" for a link to a sample digital citizenship audit.

The use of an audit, tailored to your setting, provides information that should be used to craft a digital citizenship education program for your school. The audit should include the perspectives of students, teachers, administrators, technology leaders, and parents or guardians. Each stakeholder has information that is important in gaining a full portrait of the status of misuse and abuse in the schools. Digital citizenship education based on data gathered from the school's stakeholders will result in a program that is responsive to local needs. See Figure 5.3 for the array of internal school stakeholders for digital citizenship education.

Figure 5.3   Internal School Stakeholders for Digital Citizenship Education

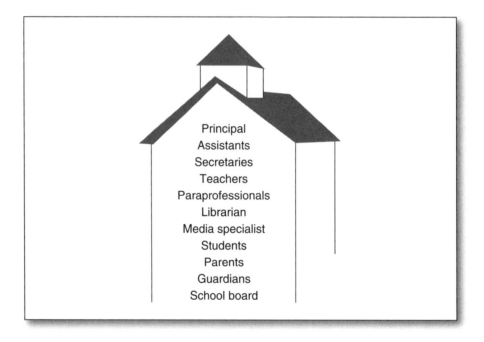

Once the audit information has been collected, a team should be appointed to translate the data into a digital citizenship education program. All stakeholders should be invited to participate in the discussion of the program's development. The support of the stakeholders is essential for successful implementation of the program (Jones, 2006).

The digital citizenship program is accompanied by acceptable use policies. Parents and students should be required to sign these policy statements as a condition of using school technology resources. Policies must be reviewed on an annual basis so that they continue to reflect the current issues in technology use (Burke, 2000; Emmans, 2000; Feinberg & Robey, 2008; Franek, 2005–2006; Hodge & Lin, 2003; Lazarus & Lipper, 1996; MacFarlane, 2007).

Civility Education

A term that is prominent in the discussion of cybersafety is *incivility.* An article by Kornblum (2007) in *USA Today* notes "online incivility [as] an increasingly hot topic" (p. 1). Incivility on the Internet, as well as the anonymity provided by blogs and social networking sites such as Facebook and MySpace (Kornblum), is apparent. The need for civility education as part of digital citizenship education is clear.

Using a foundation of rights and responsibilities, the team that examines the digital citizenship audit data must be asked to incorporate civility education into the plan for the school. Digital citizenship education and civility education must be provided for students, teachers, staff, and parents. Student education is a given in the school setting. Teacher and staff education are part of the professional development programs of schools and school districts. The reports of teachers' involvement in technology misuse and abuse as both perpetrators and victims make their education as digital citizens essential. Principals' responsibilities include the tasks noted in Figure 5.4.

Figure 5.4 Principals' Responsibilities

School Leaders Should

- Be alert to warning signs
- Seek law enforcement involvement when necessary
- Be knowledgeable about the law
- Recognize free speech and free expression

Parent Education

Parent education must be included in the process. The public media outlets flame with horror stories of students as victims or perpetrators of harassment. Stories of teachers' private activities becoming public through technology rivet attention on the news. News reports, "Live at Five," keep viewers up-to-date on the advancements in technology and its reach into the lives of students.

Administrators described the importance of parent education in the following remarks:

I'm adamant on cybersafety . . . just seeing what's out there and what can be exposed, and I think not only should we secure our kids at the network level, but we also should do consistent educating of our children, parents, students, teachers, and administrators. Even our administrators don't

know what's out there. So I think, besides securing . . . [make sure they] understand why we're blocking it and give them the skills to know what's good and what's bad.

We urge parents when they come in with kids who have been threatened in some way and it's happened at home: Our immediate response is, "Have you taken this to the police?" Because usually, they have printed something out and they bring it to school and they want us to do something, but this didn't happen at school.

Having more learning centers within our schools, to bring the parents in . . . more teaching our parents what's out there with the cyberbullying and social networking. Educating our parents on Internet safety, educating our children on Internet safety because, of course, if your parent is not a 21st Century parent, then they don't know how to protect the children.

If we bring in the younger teachers who do have the 21st Century skills, they want to use MySpace, they want to use Facebook as tools in the classroom. But are they necessarily teaching parents how to actually monitor their kids in using those tools also?

Parents may need assistance in their efforts to monitor students' behavior. Schools that sponsor parent education on issues of cyberbullying, social networking, cybersafety strategies, and monitoring online computer access strengthen the partnership that is essential as the boundaries between school and home are blurred through technology. The U.S. government has issued materials to assist parents with their role in cybersafety. *Net Cetera: Chatting With Kids About Being Online* is available at "OnGuardOnline.gov, the federal government's online safety website" (Stansbury, 2009, p. 2).

Guides for parents are available from a number of sources. The emphasis of these publications has been consistent. "The home-school connection is at the heart of a successful education system" (Lazarus & Lipper, 1996, p. 30).

Parents rely on school leaders for tips and guidelines for navigating technology issues. Because parental involvement is critical in addressing the special challenges that can emerge from technology misuse and abuse; it is in the best interest of the students and school for principals to assume leadership in this area. Principals can direct parents to valuable resources such as those included in "Principal's Exploration Agenda."

As a parent education program is developed, the following topics should be included:

- School district policies and procedures
- How to recognize and report instances of harassment and cyberbullying
- Cyberbullying and how it may be initiated at home

- How social networking sites work
- Signs a child is a victim of cyberbullying
- Parental control filtering software
- Placement of computers in the home
- Blocking access and screening usage
- Guidelines for online behavior
- Tracing emails and instant messages through Internet service providers (ISPs)
- Conversations with children and adolescents about usage and safety

Source: Feinberg and Robey (2008); Franek (2005–2006); Goddard (2008); Hodge & Lin (2003); Lazarus and Lipper (1996); MacFarlane (2007).

The best protection parents can offer their children is to teach them how to use the Internet following the rules of etiquette and the rules established by parents.

Remember: Internet etiquette, commonly known as *netiquette,* refers to the set of practices created over the years to make the Internet experience pleasant for everyone. Netiquette, like other forms of etiquette, involves matters of courtesy in communications.

Remember: The Children's Internet Protection Act (CIPA) is a federal law enacted by Congress to address concerns about access to offensive content over the Internet on school and library computers. CIPA imposes certain types of requirements on any school or library that receives funding for Internet access or internal connections from the E-rate program—a program that makes certain communications technology more affordable for eligible schools and libraries. In early 2001, the FCC issued rules implementing CIPA (Federal Communications Commission, 2009, para. 1) found on the following website: www.fcc.gov/cgb/consumerfacts/cipa.html.

ACTION AGENDA

- Use the focus questions to identify the boundaries of technology in the school.
- Develop goals based on your responses to the focus questions.
- Conduct a digital citizenship audit.
- Develop and deliver a parent education program.
- Complete the technology use guidelines survey.
- Follow the principal's exploration agenda: Explore the technology resources using the 15-minute-a-day approach.

Resources

Technology Use Guidelines

Principal's Exploration Agenda

TECHNOLOGY USE GUIDELINES

Figure 5.5 Technology Use Guidelines

1. **How often are the guidelines for technology use reviewed?**

   ❏ Each quarter   ❏ Each semester   ❏ Each year

2. **Who is involved in identifying, monitoring, and updating the guidelines?**

   ❏ Administrators   ❏ Technology specialists
   ❏ Teachers   ❏ Students
   ❏ Curriculum specialists   ❏ Parents
   ❏ Library and media personnel

3. **How is the effectiveness of the guidelines determined?**

   ❏ Number of student concerns reported
   ❏ Number of teacher concerns reported
   ❏ Number of staff concerns reported
   ❏ Number of parent concerns reported
   ❏ Comparison with technology trends related to the guidelines
   ❏ Comparison with current national technology guidelines and recent changes
   ❏ Comparison with current state technology guidelines and recent changes

4. **Who leads the review process?**

PRINCIPAL'S EXPLORATION AGENDA

Use the 15-minute-a-day approach to explore the vast resources related to technology.

The following sites are places to begin the exploration:

Websites

- Federal Bureau of Investigation: *A Parent's Guide to Internet Safety*: This site provides strategies for addressing parental concerns about Internet risks to children's safety:

  http://www.fbi.gov/publications/pguide/pguidee.htm

- Federal Bureau of Investigation: Kids' Page: This site helps children become familiar with the FBI:

  http://www.fbi.gov/fbikids.htm

- GetNetWise: This site provides examples of acceptable use policies (AUPs) for parents and children:

  http://www.getnetwise.org

- International Society for Technology in Education (ISTE): This site provides access to National Educational Technology Standards (NETS) for administrators, teachers, and students:

  http://www.iste.org/standards/aspx

- International Society for Technology in Education: Focus on Digital Citizenship: This site provides resources related to digital citizenship:

  http://www.iste.org/connect/iste-connects/blog-detail/10-08-04/Digital_Citizenship_Nurturing_the_School-Parent_Partnership.aspx

- National Center for Missing and Exploited Children: On this site you will find information on how to report illegal activity, child exploitation, and child sightings to the center:

  http://www.missingkids.com/missingkids/servlet/PublicHomeServlet?LanguageCountry=en_US&

- NetCitizens: This site has resources to help you develop acceptable use policies:

  http://sites.google.com/site/netcitizens/home/acceptable-use-policies

- Netsmartz for Kids (National Center for Missing and Exploited Children): The center supplies games and information for kids to stay safe online:

  http://www.netsmartz.org

- OnGuard Online: This site provides tips for Internet safety and protection of personal information:

  http://www.onguardonline.gov

- OnGuard Online: Cybersafety Booklet for Parents and Kids: *Net Cetera: Chatting With Kids About Being Online:* This guide is designed to help parents and kids navigate the Internet:

  http://www.ongardonline.gov/pdf/tec04.pdf

- OnGuard Online: Kids' Privacy: This site provides tips to help parents and teachers keep kids safe online:

  http://www.onguardonline.gov/topics/kids-privacy.aspx

- Safe Surfin' Foundation: The site provides safe surfing guidelines for kids on the Internet:

  http://www.sheriffs.org/programs/SafeSurfinHomePage.asp

- Search Engine Watch: This site provides tips and information about searching the web:

  http://searchenginewatch.com

- U.S. Department of Justice, Office of Justice Programs, Office of Juvenile Justice and Delinquency Prevention: This site provides Internet safety tips and rules for Internet behavior:

  http://ojjdp.gov

6 Assessment

Technology Use and Skills

The principal is responsible for *assessment*—the formative and summative evaluation of student and teacher performance as well as the schools' activities and programs. Assessments should be designed to provide instructional feedback, to monitor overall progress, and to evaluate interventions (Baker, 2003). Technology is intertwined with the assessment processes. Technology is both a tool to facilitate assessment and an aspect of the school's program that requires a place in the assessment process:

> A great challenge in the area is the pace of change in technology. We can all cite examples of buying a digital artifact (e.g., still camera, video recorder, personal digital assistant, cell phone) at a given price, only to see the next version in a month or two, with spiffier options at reduced cost. No one can keep abreast of changes if they believe they can design for every incremental platform developed for computational support. (Baker, p. 423)

TECHNOLOGY ASSESSMENT

Anderson (2004) identified three free online tools to assess students', teachers', administrators', and parents' use of technology as well as their technology skills and knowledge:

1. ProfilerPro

    The tool includes surveys for K–12 educators to be used to test technology skills and knowledge.

    http://www.profilerpro.com

2. Taking a Good Look at Instructional Technology (TAGLIT)

These surveys, designed for students, teachers, administrators, and parents, measure technology skills and how individuals use technology. To use these tools, a principal must "join the free TAGLIT Principals Executive program sponsored by the Bill and Melinda Gates Foundation, Bell South, and the software company, SAS in School" (p. 51).

http://www.testkids.com/taglit/?CFID=174181&CFTOKEN=10492200

3. The School Technology and Readiness (STaR) Chart

This survey provides results useful for planning professional development activities. The survey focuses on these questions: "Is your school using technology effectively to ensure the best possible teaching and learning? What is your school's current education technology profile? And what areas should your school focus on to improve its level of technology integration?" (p. 52).

http://www.ceoforum.org/starchart.html

The first step in the evaluation cycle is to identify the goals of evaluation. Once the goals are identified, the subjects or targets of the evaluation can be determined. When the focus of the evaluation is known, the measures and instruments of evaluation can be identified. The measures and instruments are used to gather data to determine the level of performance and goal attainment. These data are used to identify the goals for the next cycle of evaluation. The evaluation process is continuous, informed, and planned based on the goals and the data gathered through the process.

FORMATIVE EVALUATION

Formative assessment tools are available in web-based and software-based formats. The web-based tools "are online versions of traditional paper-based tests" (Villano, 2006, p. 8). A number of vendors offer these tools: SchoolNet, Scantron, Renaissance Learning, Pearson School Systems, and Harcourt Assessment (Villano).

The software-based tools include products such as Focus on Standards from Educational Testing Service. These tools are uploaded to a server or are networked to classroom computers. Handheld computers are emerging as a convenient means of conducting assessments (Villano, 2006).

Formative assessment areas include math, reading, science, social studies, and language arts. Villano (2006) cautions administrators to invest in tools "that assess all the subject areas you need to test" (p. 8).

In selecting assessment tools, it is essential to invest in tools that include a pool of current questions based on contemporary subject content, aligned with your state's standards, that assess what your district needs to assess and that provide results and reports useful to teachers and parents. The utility of these assessments is manifested in the use made of the results in assisting students in their learning needs (Villano, 2006).

Assessment tools are familiar aspects of schools. Principals are challenged to close the achievement gap. The assessment tools provide data that identify academic areas that require increased attention.

Comments from school administrators suggest the place assessment tools have in the work of the schools. One administrator reported the importance of knowing how to use the district data:

Whatever your district is using, you must be able to get in and to analyze your students' scores. Is your curriculum addressing the weaknesses that your student population, as a whole, has?

Another comment by an administrator indicated the extent of information available to principals and teachers:

You learn to use the program. I mean, most good programs will tell you exactly where your kids are, where each individual kid is in every skill set that you're trying to teach. The trick is for teachers to tie that to the actual day-to-day instruction. And I think that might be where, a lot of times, we're missing the boat—that link right there. And most programs will link that for you, if you know how to use it and pull it out. It will automatically generate your lesson plans and what you need to do to address those things. The teachers often don't take the additional step to utilize those other resources.

These comments indicate that there is significant data and direction available to teachers and principals. The key to using the data and direction is the individual's willingness to use the resources made available through the technology.

Another administrator described principals as "being forced to use technology." As the focus on student achievement becomes more prominent, attention to school-site data increases. The window to the data is through technology. In the following administrator's comments, the importance of technology as a means of ready access to student achievement data is evident:

One of the ways that principals are being forced into the use of technology is through the data collection. I don't know of any state anywhere that is not relying heavily upon data, number one, to determine AYP at

the state level, but at the district level you've got to determine it, and then at the school-site level you've got to determine it. What you're trying to look at is, do you have strong or weak teachers? Strong or weak subjects? Strong or weak grade levels?

An administrator described the use of technology to identify strengths and weaknesses:

We use technology to help determine where our strengths and weaknesses are within classrooms, at grade levels, at school sites, and even across the district. Looking at a curriculum you've adopted, you can see that you've got a weakness in an area; then, you can use these technology tools to help you determine, is it a problem with the curriculum or is it a problem with the application of the curriculum?

CLASSROOM ASSESSMENTS

In addition to district use of technology to monitor student achievement data, teachers have adopted technology tools as a means of formative and summative assessment. One principal described the growth of interest in technology tools for assessment:

We delivered professional development to the faculty about CPS,* kind of gauging their interest: "Would this be something you'd be willing to try in your classroom, knowing that we're studying formative and summative assessment?" You can gather data about formative assessment. The response was a pretty strong "yes," so we're going to go with four more sets that are able to be checked out for other teachers. Then, if the demand is as high as the survey indicated it would be, we'll probably look to purchase another four or five sets for the upcoming school year.

*CPS: Classroom Performance System. A system designed to engage students in classroom activities.

Another administrator noted the use of clickers and digital slates as tools teachers use to assess student understanding during a lesson. The information generated through these technology tools can be used to adapt lessons to the level of student understanding.

ASSESSMENT CHALLENGES

The assessment movement, fueled by achievement data, has been aided by technology tools. One administrator, however, described an assessment challenge often voiced within the education community:

Our assessments do not do a good job of assessing critical thinking. You know, those higher-level thinking skills. And it's tough to write an assessment for higher-level thinking skills to really know how your kids have thought it through. That is something we're really feeling our way through. You want your kids to do a blog on a piece of literature—how are you going to assess that? You can count how many times the kids submit something on the blog or respond to somebody else, but is it a quality response? How do you show an exemplary model? Because a lot of stuff in blogs is junk.

The skills cited by this administrator are a reminder of the importance of Bloom's revised taxonomy (Anderson & Krathwohl, 2001) in the 21st Century school.

TEACHERS' USE OF TECHNOLOGY

Administrators responded to questions about teachers' use of technology as part of instruction. One administrator said,

We have a part in our evaluation that is heavy on professional development, and sometimes, a principal will require a technology goal—so they have to teach themselves and work on something that allows technology to be integrated.

Another administrator reported,

This is part of your evaluation; this is what you're going to have to do. . . . You don't let them age out of the system, because you have a lot of kids who are missing out. . . . You give them every opportunity to improve and rise to the occasion, and if that doesn't happen, then they may have to leave.

PRINCIPALS' USE OF TECHNOLOGY

An administrator described the necessity for principals to use technology:

I had some principals who were very good at technology, and I had some who just flat refused to do it. They just wouldn't do it. And if it's part of their evaluation and they don't do it and they continue not to do it, then they need to go away, because they can't, in most cases, make AYP. You can't improve student achievement without using data. And if you're not improving student achievement and you're not making AYP, then you can't be a principal. If there's not any improvement seen, then you've got to go.

DIGITAL AGE ASSESSMENT

Tuttle (2007) notes, "Assembling an *e-portfolio,* or electronic portfolio, is an excellent method for assessing students' progress toward school, state, or national academic standards, as well as 21st Century skills" (p. 22). Portfolios are a form of assessment that goes beyond the results of a standardized test. The portfolio provides an opportunity to demonstrate a comprehensive, in-depth collection of work for a specified time frame. Portfolios have become standard features of teacher and administrator preparation programs. When linked to goals, program expectations, and performance standards, and assessed based on a rubric, they are useful demonstration products. Using portfolios in elementary and secondary schools provides opportunities for students to showcase the technology skills they have mastered as well as to demonstrate their mastery of curricular objectives:

> E-portfolios support 21st Century skills in a variety of ways. Self-assessment becomes a regular part of learning as students frequently select or reevaluate which of their work is the best evidence of their skills and strive to create even better evidence in their future assignments. Formative assessment also plays a key role through regular teacher feedback. (Tuttle, 2007, p. 23)

Teachers can use different technology tools to determine mastery and understanding of class material. Clickers have become prevalent in classrooms as a means of checking student understanding of class work. As students have greater access to online resources, they can respond to Zoomerang or Moodle quizzes that allow teachers to determine student understanding of instruction. Teachers may have access to course-management systems, such as

Blackboard, that provide survey tools (e.g., HotChalk). These systems allow teachers to provide explanations and in-depth feedback to students (Tuttle, 2008, para. 6). Google Docs (i.e., documents, spreadsheets, presentations, and forms) are free and easy to use. Principals and teachers can exchange information. Teachers can advise students on how to revise documents. Administrators, teachers, and students can collect and collate data using the forms.

"To develop elementary students' reading skills, teachers can record how many words they read in a given number of minutes over numerous weeks. After they finish reading, teachers record in a log or a PDA, tablet computer, or desktop computer" (Tuttle, 2008, para. 6).

Baker (2003) describes tools for instructional feedback such as "assessments to monitor overall progress and assessments for evaluating particular interventions" (p. 424). Feedback to students should be consistent so that students can benefit from the data provided through assessments. Parents, too, seek feedback about student's performance. Parents who are provided with feedback are able to assist and encourage students in their school work. Teachers should be encouraged to explore the range of feedback tools that are available based on the assessments used in conjunction with instruction.

Principals who work in schools that offer online classes must be prepared to evaluate the teachers of these classes. Borja (2005) reported that data concerning the teacher can be collected online. These data include "how often and how long the teacher spends online on any given day, the contents of email messages and phone calls, the teacher's online grade book, student and parent feedback, and archived, interactive whiteboard discussions" (p. 8).

Other feedback tools teachers may choose to use for explanations and feedback include Wikis, podcasts, and spreadsheets that can be used to keep students informed of their progress in class. These and other tools are significant because they increase and enhance the communication with students (and parents) about the students' learning needs and progress. As the tools become more prevalent and user-friendly, teachers become more adept in using them. More feedback about student progress encourages a greater focus on the teaching and learning process.

ACTION AGENDA

- Use the three free online assessment tools to determine teachers', students', administrators', and parents' technology skills and knowledge, as well as to plan professional development activities.
- Explore technology tools such as Wikis, podcasts, Google Docs, Zoomerang, Moodle, clickers, and e-portfolios.

Part III

Questions and Reflections

7 Questions and Reflections

Two aspects of technology tools are of critical importance to principals. One, what technology tools does your school have? Two, what technology tools should you have?

The proliferation of technology is exciting and astonishing. The caveat: What is new today is soon replaced or enhanced by another product. So one must be realistic about the built-in obsolescence of technology.

The analogy of the development of the electric lightbulb is instructive. The earliest lightbulbs were built with a filament designed to last forever. However, in a capitalist economy, it is difficult for a manufacturer to be a financially successful producer of lightbulbs if there is never a need for a replacement bulb. Built-in obsolescence is key to a financially successful manufacturing enterprise—as is innovation.

How many cell phones have you owned and replaced? Remember rotary-dial phones? Probably not! They seemed to endure longer than cell phones do. Compare your first cell phone with your current cell phone. How many features does your cell phone have? How many children in your school have cell phones? How old are those children?

Keep these analogies in mind as you survey the technology in your school. What exists? How old is it? Who uses it? Can you operate it?

How do individuals in the school learn to operate the technology? Does someone teach the teachers and administrators to operate technology?

Who teaches students to operate technology? How do students learn to use cell phones and iPods? Who teaches them text messaging skills? Who teaches students how to use Facebook, Twitter, or MySpace?

Do you have access to the following tools and devices? (See Figure 7.1.) Do you use the tools and devices, if you have access?

Figure 7.1 Access and Use

Access and Use of Common Tools and Devices				
	Do you have?		Do you use?	
	Yes (✓)	No (✓)	Yes (✓)	No (✓)
Facebook				
MySpace				
Twitter				
Text Messaging				
iPod				
iTouch				
iPhone				
Blackberry				
Kindle				
iPad				
Nook				

Do students have handheld Internet access? Are students permitted to use their handheld devices during school hours?

Technology resources often found in schools include the following:

- Interactive whiteboards
- Clickers
- Digital cameras
- Video cameras
- Computers
- Wireless connections

Are these resources available to all teachers and in all classrooms? And are they being used?

These few resources can be key to fostering collaborative learning experiences for students. Remember, if we are preparing students with 21st Century skills, we need to focus on the following:

- Adaptability
- Analytical skills
- Collaboration
- Creativity

- Critical thinking
- Curiosity
- Effective speaking
- Effective writing
- Global awareness
- Information literacy
- Innovation
- Media fluency
- Problem solving
- Synthesis (McLeod, 2010)

Designing learning experiences to foster these skills can be facilitated through technology, if teachers are open to using the tools and motivated to do so. The principal is key to opening the door to technology use. Remember, the students have already embraced the tools. Students have the skills.

TECHNOLOGY TRENDS

The future of education will be enriched by the 2010 trends noted in *THE Journal* (McCrea, 2009):

- eBooks will continue to proliferate.
- Netbook functionality will continue to grow.
- More teachers will use interactive whiteboards.
- Personal devices will infiltrate the classroom.
- Technology will enable tailored curricula. (pp. 1–2)

Consider the ramifications of Carr's (2008) analysis of the impact of the Internet on how we read and think. Prowling the Internet becomes the enemy of reading by diminishing literacy and reducing attention span. Carr wrote, "Once I was a scuba diver in the sea of words. Now I zip along the surface like a guy on a jet ski" (para. 4). The more we use the web, the more we have to fight to stay focused on long pieces of writing. "We may well be in the midst of a sea change in the way we read and think" (Carr, para. 7).

The following messages are reminders of how we write, communicate, and decode. A sea change is occurring, but it is not the first.

Morse Code

Morse code was an important means of communication in the past. It was first used in 1836 with the production of the first working telegraph. Through the years, it has provided a means of reliable communication without the need for special equipment (Agar, 2010) (Figure 7.2 on next page.)

Morse Code Sample Text

Figure 7.2   Morse Code Sample

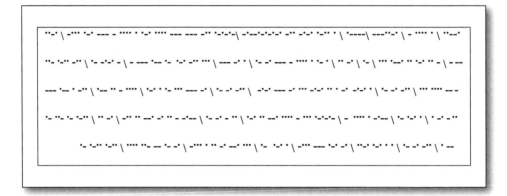

Translation:

All human beings are born free and equal in dignity and rights. They are endowed with reason and conscience and should act towards one another in a spirit of brotherhood. (Article 1 of the *Universal Declaration of Human Rights,* 1948)

Gregg Shorthand

Shorthand was taught as an important note-taking skill in the past. In 1888, John Robert Gregg published two pamphlets titled *Gregg Shorthand,* and the system was published in book form in 1897. Because it was easy to learn, read, and write, coupled with the capability of speed and accuracy, Gregg shorthand quickly became the standard shorthand system of schools in the United States (Gregg, 1919).

Gregg Shorthand Message

Figure 7.3   Gregg Shorthand Sample

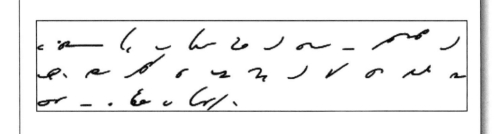

Translation:

All human beings are born free and equal in dignity and rights. They are endowed with reason and conscience and should act towards one another in a spirit of brotherhood. (Article 1 of the *Universal Declaration of Human Rights,* 1948)

Text Messaging

In 2011, text messages and tweets are common forms of communication. Also known as *Short Message Service*, text messaging allows you to send a message from one cell phone to another by accessing the recipient's cell phone number.

Text Message

Figure 7.4   Text Messaging Sample

Translation:

Hi,
   Too good to be true. Congratulations. What do you think about dinner? Talk to you later. Love you.

Twitter

Twitter allows you to discover what is happening right now with anyone with whom you connect, anywhere they are.

Twitter Message

Figure 7.5   Twitter Sample

Thanks Dan and classmates–it was a great class.
6:46 PM Aug 8th, 2008 via twhirl

This *is* the 21st Century. To be a principal in the 21st Century school demands leadership of technology. To be a leader of technology requires a willingness to learn, flexibility, and the capacity to accept change as a constant factor. Adaptability and acceptance of ambiguity are essential. Because technology changes continuously, there is no menu of technology must dos and must haves. Instead, leaders of technology must be lifelong learners and explorers of the new, the exciting, and the useful in technology. And as you explore,

Remember the five-year-old!

References

Agar, S. (2010). *Morse code.* Retrieved on July 29, 2010, from http://www.omniglot.com

Anderson, L. W., & Krathwohl, D. R. (Eds.) (with Airasian, P. W., Cruikshank, K. A., Mayer, R. E., Pintrich, P. R., Raths, J., & Wittrock, M. C.). (2001). *A taxonomy for learning, teaching, and assessing: A revision of Bloom's taxonomy of educational objectives* (Complete ed.). New York: Longman.

Anderson, M. A. (2004). Does your tech program measure up? Three online tools to assess your school's performance. *School Library Journal, 12,* 50–52. Retrieved from http://www.schoollibraryjournal.com/slj/printissuecurrentissue/871209-427/does_your_tech_program_measure.html.csp

Ashmore, R. W., & Herman, B. M. (2006, May). Abuse in cyberspace. *School Administrator, 63*(5), 33–36.

Baker, E. L. (2003). Reflections on technology-enhanced assessment. *Assessment in Education, 10*(3), 421–424.

Bauer, J., & Kenton, J. (2005). Toward technology integration in the schools: Why it isn't happening. *Journal of Technology and Teacher Education, 13*(4), 519–546.

Borja, R. R. (2005, August 10). Evaluating online teachers is largely a virtual task. *Education Week, 24*(44), 8. Available from http://www.edweek.org

Bray, B. (2003). *Stages of concern about technology use* [Chart]. Available from http://my-ecoach.com

Brockmeier, L. L., Sermon, J. M., & Hope, W. C. (2005, June). Principals' relationship with computer technology. *NASSP Bulletin, 89*(643), 45–63.

Brown, B. (2007, August). *Factors that contribute to the transition of teachers' uses of technology from administrative tasks to instructional integration.* Paper presented at the Annual Meeting of the National Council of Professors of Educational Administration, San Diego, CA.

Burke, J. (2000). *Rights, risks and responsibilities: Students and the Internet.* Available from ERIC database. (ED459694)

Bushweller, K. (1996). How mighty is your wizard? *American School Board Journal, 183*(5), a14–a16.

Carr, N. (2008, July/August). *Is Google making us stupid?* Retrieved from http://www.theatlantic.com/magazine/archive/2008/07/is-google-making-us-stupid/6868

Cooley, V. E., & Reitz, R. J. (1997). Lessons learned in creating a program. *Kappa Delta Pi, 34*(1), 4–9.

Corder, G. W., Marshall, I., Lineweaver, L., & McIntyre, P. (2008, January). Teachers take the lead. *Principal Leadership, 8*(5), 27–29.

Davis, M. R. (2008, June 4). Help wanted: Finding the right IT worker. *Education Week's Digital Directions, 2*(2), 30. Advance online publication. Retrieved October 18, 2009, from http://www.edweek.org/dd/articles/2008/06/04/04hiring_web.h01.html

Emmans, C. (2000, Spring). Internet ethics. *Technos, 9*(1), 34–36.

eSchool News & SchoolDude.com (with Consortium of School Networking). (2009). *Executive summary: 2008 survey: The Unique Challenges Facing the IT Professional in K–12 Education.* Retrieved from http://marketing.schooldude.com/marketing/it/2008-k12-it-survey-exec-summary.pdf

Federal Communications Commission. (2009). *Children's Internet Protection Act.* Retrieved from http://www.fcc.gov/cgb/consumerfacts/cipa.html

Feinberg, T., & Robey, N. (2008, September). Cyberbullying. *Principal Leadership, 9*(1), 10–14.

Franek, M. (2005–2006, December/January). Foiling cyberbullies in the new Wild West. *Educational Leadership, 63*(4), 39–43.

Frazier, M. K. (2003). *The technology coordinator in K–12 school districts: The research, development, and validation of a technology leader's guide.* Available from ProQuest Digital Dissertations. (UMI No. 3100547)

GetNetWise. (n.d.). *Tools for families.* Retrieved 2009 from http://www.getnetwise.org/tools/toolscontracts.shtml

Glickman, C. D., Gordon, S. P., & Ross-Gordon, J. M. (2006). *Supervision and instructional leadership: A developmental approach* (7th ed.). Boston: Pearson.

Goddard, C. (2008, March). Cyber world bullying. *Education Digest, 73*(7), 4–9.

Grady, M. (2004). *20 Biggest mistakes principals make and how to avoid them.* Thousand Oaks, CA: Corwin.

Grady, M. L., & LeSourd, S. J. (1989–1990). Principals' attitudes toward visionary leadership. *The High School Journal, 73*(2), 103–110.

Gregg, J. R. (1919). *Gregg shorthand: A light-line phonography for the million.* New York: Gregg.

Hodge, L., & Lin, H. (2003, April/May). A combined strategy for Internet safety. *Our Children, 28*(6), 11–12.

Johnson, D. (2005, May). What does a tech-savvy administrator look like? *School Administrator, 62*(5), 1–2.

Jones, P. J. (2006). Resources for promoting online citizenship. *Educational Leadership, 63*(4), 41.

Kornblum, J. (2007, July 31). Rudeness, threats make the web a cruel world: Sites wrestle with balancing free speech, civility. *USA Today,* pp. 1, 2.

Lazarus, W., & Lipper, L. (1996). *The parents' guide to the information superhighway: Rules and tools for families online.* Retrieved from ERIC database. (ED401872)

Lesisko, L. J. (2004). *Characteristics and responsibilities of technology coordinators employed in public school districts in the Commonwealth of Pennsylvania.* Available from ProQuest Digital Dissertations. (UMI No. 3167654)

Lesisko, L. J. (2005, March). *The K–12 technology coordinator.* Paper presented at the Annual Meeting of the Eastern Educational Research Association, Sarasota, FL.

LeSourd, S. J., & Grady, M. L. (1989–1990). Visionary attributes in principals' description of their leadership. *The High School Journal, 73*(2), 111–117.

LeSourd, S. J., Tracz, S., & Grady, M. L. (1992). Attitude toward visionary leadership. *Journal of School Leadership, 2*(1), 34–44.

MacFarlane, M. A. (2007). *Misbehavior in cyberspace.* Retrieved from http://www
.education.com/reference/article/misbehavior-cyberspace-rise-social

Mayo, N., Kajs, L., & Tanguma, J. (2005, September). Longitudinal study of
technology training to prepare future teachers. *Educational Research Quarterly,
29*(1), 3–15.

McCrea, B. (2009). *5 K–12 technology trends for 2010.* Retrieved from http://the
journal.com/articles/2009/12/10/5-k12-technology-trends-for-2010.aspx?sc_
lang=en

McLeod, S. (2010). *2010–2011 SAI technology leadership training: Phase 1, day 1:
Two big shifts and one big problem* [PowerPoint slides]. Retrieved January 12,
2011, from http://uceacastle.wikispaces.com

McPherson, S., Wizer, D., & Pierrel, E. (2006, February). Technology academies.
Learning & Leading with Technology, 33(5), 26–31.

Office of Educational Technology. (2010, March 5). *Transforming American education:
Learning powered by technology: National education technology plan 2010,
executive summary* [Draft]. Available from www.ed.gov/tech/netp-2010

Partnership for 21st Century Skills. (2009). *Framework for 21st century learning.*
Available from http://www.p21.org/documents/P21_Framework.pdf

Patton, C. (2006, June). Education in hand: Conquering cyberphobia, one staffer at
a time. *District Administration,* 10–14.

Place, R. A., & Lesisko, L. J. (2005, October). *Hiring the best qualified technology
coordinator: A Pennsylvania perspective.* Paper presented at the PASA-PSBA
School Leadership Conference, Hershey, PA.

Ribble, M. S., & Bailey, G. D. (2004). *Monitoring technology misuse & abuse.*
Retrieved from http://www.digitalcitizenship.net/uploads/T.H.E.JournalArticle.pdf

Rogers, E. R. (2003). *Diffusion of innovations* (5th ed.). New York: Free Press.

Stansbury, M. (2009). *Feds release cyber safety booklet.* Retrieved from http://www
.eschoolnews.com/2009/12/16/ftc-doe-release-cybersafety-booklet

Sutton, S. (2009, February). School solutions for cyberbullying. *Principal Leadership,
(9)*6, 38–40, 42.

Taylor, K. R. (2008, May). Cyberbullying: Is there anything schools can do? *Principal
Leadership, 8*(9), 60–62.

Technology & Learning. (2008, May). More than a techie. *Technology & Learning,
28*(10), 1–2.

Technology & Learning. (n.d.). *Fundamentals of K–12 technology programs: Issue 3.
Educational technology leadership: The key to progress and change.* Available
from www.techlearning.com/K12/Fundamentals

Technology Standards for School Administrators (TSSA) Collaborative. (2001).
Technology standards for school administrators. Retrieved from http://www
.ncrtec.org/pd/tssa/tssa.pdf

Tinker v. Des Moines Independent Community School District, 393 U.S. 503 (1969).

Trotter, A. (1997, November 10). A test of leadership. *Education Week, 17*(11), 30.

Tuttle, H. G. (2007, February). Digital-age assessment. *Technology & Learning, 27*(7),
22–24.

Tuttle, H. G. (2008). *Part 1: Digital age assessment.* Retrieved from http://www
.techlearning.com/article/8592

Villano, M. (2006, January). Assessing formative assessment: Get the skinny on
technology-based assessment systems. *Technology & Learning, 26,* 8.

What is 21st century education? (2004). Retrieved April 7, 2010, from http://www.21stcenturyschools.com/what_is_21st_century_education.htm

Williams, S., & Kingham, M. (2003). Infusion of technology into the curriculum. *Journal of Instructional Psychology, 30*(3), 178–184.

Wolinsky, A. (2008, July). Realizing educational technology's potential in the face of Internet safety issues. *Multimedia & Internet Schools, 15*(4), 26–30.

Wright, R. J., & Lesisko, L. J. (2007, February). *The preparation and role of technology leadership for schools.* Paper presented at the Annual Meeting of the Eastern Educational Research Association, Clearwater, FL.

Index

Academic degrees, 49
Acceptable use policies, 72–73
Agar, S., 95
Anderson, L. W., 87
Anderson, M. A., 83
Ashmore, R. W., 70
Assessment
  challenges for, 87
  classroom, 86
  definition of, 83
  digital age, 88–89
  electronic portfolios, 88
  formative, 84–86
  goals of, 84
  online classes, 89
  technology, 83–84
Audit, 74

Bailey, G. D., 73
Baker, E. L., 83, 89
Bauer, J., 33
Blogs, 19–20
Borja, R. R., 89
Bray, B., 63
Brockmeier, L. L., 8
Brown, B., 33
Burke, J., 74
Bushweller, K., 48

Calendar, 14
Carr, N., 95
Cell phones, 70
Certifications
  director of instructional
    technology, 47
  technology specialist, 46
  vendor, 49
Change, resistance to, 13

Children's Internet Protection Act, 77
Civility education, 75
Classroom assessments, 86
Classroom learning, 32
Collaborative learning, 94–95
Concerns Based Adoption Model, 62
Cooley, V. E., 9, 15
Corder, G. W., 32
Cyberbullying, 65, 67, 70, 72
Cybersafety
  boundaries issues, 70
  challenges for, 70–71
  filtering, 71–73
  governmental resources, 76
  incivility, 75
  parent education in, 75–77
  pornography, 70–71
Cybersafety leadership
  civility education, 75
  digital citizenship education, 73–74
  parent education, 75–77
  principal's role in, 73

Davis, M. R., 46
Digital citizenship education, 73–74
Director of education technology, 47
Director of instructional
  technology, 47–49
Displays, 10–11

Educational Testing Service, 84
Electronic portfolios, 88
Emmans, C., 74
Evaluation. *See also* Assessment
  formative, 84–86
  goals of, 84
Exploration agenda for principals,
  19–21, 43–44, 57, 81

Families, 8–9
Feedback, instructional, 89
Feinberg, T., 67, 74, 77
Filtering, 71–73
Formative evaluation, 84–86
Franek, M., 65, 74, 77
Frazier, M. K., 48
Free speech, 72

Generational shift, 34–39
Glickman, C. D., 31
Goals
    attainment of, 37
    of principal, 8–10
Goddard, C., 77
Gordon, S. P., 31
Grady, M. L., 8
Gregg, J. R., 96
Gregg Shorthand, 96–97

Herman, B. M., 70
Hodge, L., 74, 77
Hope, W. C., 8
Human capital
    list of, 12
    staff, 10
    students. See Student(s)
    teachers. See Teachers
    technology specialist.
        See Technology specialist

Incentives for teachers, 31–32
Incivility, 75
Instructional feedback, 89
Internet, 77, 95

Johnson, D., 9
Jones, P. J., 74

Kajs, L., 32
Kenton, J., 33
Kingham, M., 32
Kornblum, J., 75
Krathwohl, D. R., 87

Lazarus, W., 74, 76–77
Leadership
    cybersafety. See Cybersafety
        leadership

guidelines for, 16
    technology. See Technology
        leadership team
Lesisko, L. J., 46–47, 47–49, 49
LeSourd, S. J., 8
Lineweaver, L., 32
Lipper, L., 74, 76–77

MacFarlane, M.A., 65, 74, 77
Marshall, I., 32
Mayo, N., 32
McCrea, B., 95
McIntyre, P., 32
McLeod, S., 95
McPherson, S., 33
Morse code, 95–96

National Education Technology Plan
    2010, 15, 26–29
National technology standards, 8, 15
Need-based approach to professional
    development, 67
Netiquette, 77
Network administrator, 47–48

Online classes, 89

Parents
    acceptable use policies signed by,
        73–74
    cybersafety education for, 75–77
Patton, C., 33
Photo displays, 10–11
Pierrel, E., 33
Place, R. A., 47–49
Pornography, 70–71
Principal
    exploration agenda, 19–21, 43–44,
        57, 81
    goals of, 8–10
    monitoring of goal attainment
        by, 37
    professional development of, 14–15
    resources obtained by, 15
    school safety role of, 69
    school setting assessments by, 36
    self-assessment form for, 18
    support for technology use by, 10–11
    tasks for, 7–8

technology leadership team and, 50, 52–53
technology use by, 9–10, 52, 85, 88
vision of, 8–10
Productivity and Professional Practice Standard, 9
Professional development
    acceptable use policies, 72
    administrator involvement in, 68
    agenda for, 65–67
    model of, 65–66
    need-based approach, 67
    principal, 14–15
    reliance on outside experts for, 11–12
    student learning benefits, 14
    teacher-to-teacher, 32, 36, 61–68
    technology use, 11–14
ProfilerPro, 83
Progress reports, 14

Reitz, R. J., 9, 15
Resistance to change, 13
Resources
    cybersafety, 76
    principal's role in obtaining, 15
    technology, 15, 94
Ribble, M. S., 73
Robey, N., 67, 74, 77
Rogers, E. R., 32, 61
Ross-Gordon, J. M., 31
RSS feeds, 19

School
    director of education technology, 47–49
    director of instructional technology, 47–49
    generational shift in, 34–39
    principal's assessment of, 36
    technology leadership team in, 53
    technology resources in, 94
School safety
    cyberbullying, 65, 67, 70, 72
    principal's role in, 69
School Technology and Readiness Chart, 84
School website, 11
Self-assessments, 18
Sermon, J. M., 8

Short message service, 97
Shorthand, 96–97
Social networking sites, 70, 72
Software, 44
Staff meetings, 10
Stansbury, M., 76
Student(s)
    acceptable use policies signed by, 73–74
    civility education for, 75
    collaborative learning experiences for, 94–95
    cyberbullying of, 65, 67, 70, 72
Student achievement
    technology tools used to track, 14
    technology used to facilitate, 8–9
Support, Management, and Operations standard, 9
Sutton, S., 73

Taking a Good Look at Instructional Technology, 84
Tanguma, J., 32
Taylor, K. R., 70
Teachers
    appraisal of, 13–14
    digital literacy goals for, 65
    generational shift, 34–39
    incentives for, 31–32
    modeling of technology use by, 12
    of online classes, 89
    principal's showcasing of technology use to, 10
    professional development for, 61–68
    technology knowledge of, principal's assessment of, 64
    technology use by, 10, 32–34, 42, 61, 87
    tech-savvy, 12, 33
    training for, 31
    veteran, 34–39
Technology
    acceptable use policies, 72–73
    boundaries of, 69–70
    ongoing replacement of, 93
    in schools, 94
    trends in, 95–98
Technology coordinator, 47–48
Technology leaders, 46

Technology leadership team
  conversations with, 52–53
  decision making by, 50–51
  location of, 53–54
  members of, 50
  principal's involvement with,
    50, 52–53
  role of, 50
Technology specialist
  academic degrees of, 49
  certification of, 46
  checklist for, 56
  qualifications of, 46–50
  role of, 45–46
  titles for, 46
Technology Standards for School
  Administrators, 9, 15, 22–26
Technology tools
  implementation leadership model
    for, 13
  new types of, 13
  student achievement tracked
    using, 14
Technology use
  assessment of, 83–84
  Concerns Based Adoption Model,
    62–63
  displays to promote, 10–11
  guidelines for, 80
  implementation of, 37
  in instructional practices, 38–39
  modeling of, 9–10, 12
  photo displays to promote, 10–11

by principals, 9–11, 52, 85, 88
  professional development in,
    11–14
  resources for, 15
  showcasing of, 10, 12
  stages of concern about, 62–63
  teacher modeling of, 12
  by teachers, 10, 32–34, 42, 87
Tech-savvy teachers, 12
Text messages, 97
Textbooks, 61
Tinker v. Des Moines Independent
  Community School District, 70
Tracz, S., 8
Trotter, A., 9–10
Tuttle, H. G., 88–89
Twenty-first-century learning, 3
Twitter, 97

Vendor certifications, 49
Veteran teachers, 34–39
Villano, M., 84–85
Vision, of principal as technology
  leader, 8–10

Websites
  as resources, 20–21
  school, 11
  technology-related, 43–44, 57
Williams, S., 32
Wizer, D., 33
Wolinsky, A., 70
Wright, R. J., 46–47, 49

CORWIN

A SAGE Company

The Corwin logo—a raven striding across an open book—represents the union of courage and learning. Corwin is committed to improving education for all learners by publishing books and other professional development resources for those serving the field of PreK–12 education. By providing practical, hands-on materials, Corwin continues to carry out the promise of its motto: **"Helping Educators Do Their Work Better."**

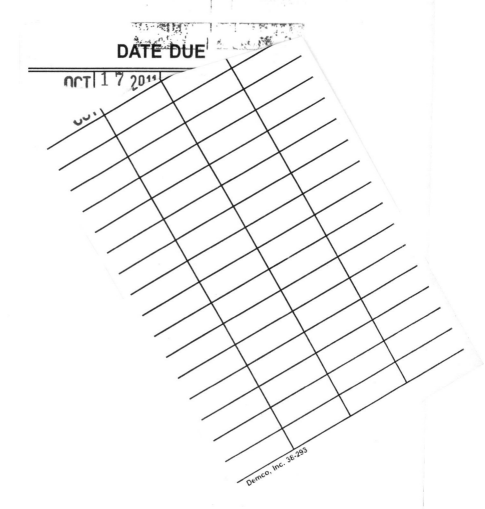